BIBLICAL CHURCH GROWTH

How You Can Work with God
to Build a Faithful Church

Gary L. McIntosh

Baker Books

A Division of Baker Book House Co
Grand Rapids, Michigan 49516

© 2003 by Gary L. McIntosh

Published by Baker Books
a division of Baker Book House Company
P.O. Box 6287, Grand Rapids, MI 49516-6287
www.bakerbooks.com

Printed in the United States of America

Library of Congress Cataloging-in-Publication Data
McIntosh, Gary, 1947–
    Biblical church growth : how you can work with God to build a faithful church / Gary L. McIntosh.
        p.   cm.
    Includes bibliographical references.
    ISBN 0-8010-9156-X (pbk.)
    1. Church growth. 2. Church growth—Biblical teaching. I. Title.
BV652.25.M3157 2003
254′ .5—dc21   200300643

Dedicated to

Donald A. McGavran
1897–1990

Father of Church Growth

Contents

Preface

Boat races in Denver, Colorado, are not very common, but a few years ago some youth pastors in that city hosted a boat race as a way to raise the morale of their youth groups. To participate in the Great Denver Boat Race, each of the youth groups had to follow three simple rules. First, each group had to select a team of two people to ride in its boat. Second, each boat had to be powered by human energy; hence, no gasoline motors or electric motors or sails were allowed. Third, each youth group had to build its own boat . . . out of milk cartons!

As the youth pastors shared the idea with their different youth groups, enthusiasm grew quickly. Each group began to design its boat, while at the same time recruiting church members to save used milk cartons for collection at church. Once enough milk cartons were collected and a boat design was agreed on, the building process began.

The wax surface of each milk carton was carefully scraped off, and then the opening was stapled shut to trap air inside. Different sized cartons were selected to fit the shape of the particular boat design. Once a test fit of the milk cartons was completed, they were glued together to form the bottom of the boat. Some milk cartons were used to make seats. Others formed sides to keep water from splashing into the boat.

On the day of the great boat race, more than twenty pickup trucks carrying the boats backed up to the edge of the shore. Each boat was carefully lifted out of the truck bed and placed gently into the water. Some of the boats looked something like rowboats, a few were shaped more like canoes, and one appeared to be designed like a Mississippi paddleboat. By the time of the race, the shore was lined with parents, youth group members, invited friends, and curious people who were just passing by.

At the appointed time, the boat crews put on their life jackets and proceeded to get their boats in line for the start of the race. Each boat was launched at the firing of a starter's pistol. The goal was to reach the center of the lake, go around a buoy, and return to the shore in the shortest amount of time.

Bang! The starter's pistol sounded and the first boat began making its way out to the middle of the lake. At one-minute intervals each succeeding boat was given the same signal and started on its one-mile journey.

After all the boats were on their way and a few were just beginning to head toward shore, one person on the shore, who was watching through binoculars, shouted, "What's that?" Instantly everyone on the shore began looking intensely, trying to see what was creating such curiosity.

To everyone's surprise, milk cartons were coming loose from the boats and drifting away. A few of the boats lost so many milk cartons that the crews slowly sank into the water. Some boats were able to make it back to shore, but most were not completely intact. Only one boat, the winner, made it back with all its milk cartons in place.

The Great Denver Boat Race is an interesting example of what often happens with churches. On the surface each boat looked like it was capable of making the trip around the buoy and back to shore. As the waves hit the boats and water soaked into the milk cartons, however, it became apparent that some boats were constructed much better than others.

In a similar way, churches look pretty much the same on the outside. Nearly all churches have worship services, programs for various age groups, buildings in which to meet, and numerous other similarities. Yet not all churches are equally healthy. Some churches exude life-giving vitality, while others struggle along searching for direction. Some churches experience biblical church growth, and others do not. Why is this so? Why do some churches grow and others don't?

That is the central issue explored in *Biblical Church Growth*. It is a question that was first addressed by Donald McGavran, the father of church growth, when he served as a missionary in India. During a missionary career that lasted three decades, he prayed, studied, and researched this question. When he began to share his discoveries, he found both acceptance and rejection of his ideas. Today he is considered by many to have been the premier missionary strategist of our time. Unfortunately, however, most pastors and church leaders no longer read his books and articles.[1]

What most pastors and church leaders know of church growth comes from popular authors who sometimes derive their ideas from sources other than the Bible. McGavran, on the other hand, was a biblical missiologist. He coined the term *church growth* as a synonym for effective evangelism, which he believed included winning converts to Christ and helping them become responsible members of local congregations. While he used modern research to enhance his understanding, the core of his insights arose from his understanding of God's authoritative Word.

You will find the fingerprints of Donald McGavran throughout *Biblical Church Growth*. In most places I have not provided documentation or footnotes tied directly to McGavran. It would have been too cumbersome to do so, as my thinking has been so shaped by his that it would be difficult at times to separate the two. However, those who know his writing will see his shadow lurking in many places in this book. Each chapter contains McGavran quotes and a prayer, which give insight into his views of church growth. Responsibility for this book and the ideas presented are solely mine, but as one of McGavran's students, I walk in his shadow.

By using the word *biblical,* I do not mean to imply that previous books written on this topic are not biblically based. I use the word *biblical* to make the point that, contrary to popular opinion, church growth is not based on sociology, marketing, or demographics. Church growth is a biblical concept, exploding from the life-giving nature of God. Unfortunately, during the years when church growth first became a recognized paradigm for church ministry, many writers assumed that its biblical foundation was well-known. At the time, most church growth authors wrote about practical issues concerning church growth, without laying a biblical foundation. Time has demonstrated that many people did not, and do not, understand the biblical foundation for church growth. Hence, *Biblical Church Growth* will focus on the biblical foundation that has often been lacking in previous church growth literature. It is beyond the scope of this book to try to nuance church growth's biblical foundation for every church, denomination, or theological system. That I must leave to each individual reader. In addition, I have sought to walk a thin line between writing an academic theological tome and a practical popular work. Whether I accomplished this task, the reader must decide. No doubt some readers will wish for more theological depth, while others will wish for more practical help. I do ask for your indulgence in this regard.

Finally, since it is God's will that lost men and women, boys and girls, be found, reconciled to God, and brought into responsible membership in Christian churches, it is my prayer that *Biblical Church Growth* will be a helpful book to pastors and church leaders as they faithfully invest in effective ministry by using biblical church growth principles.

ONE

Searching for Faithfulness

We are not called to create a static ministry for static Churches content to remain at their present size in the midst of millions of the winnable. We are called to create a ministry which will keep growing Churches growing and start non-growing Churches on the road of great growth.

Donald A. McGavran

The wet chill of fall bit my face as I walked up the driveway toward the concrete block church building. Fewer than fifty short steps from the parsonage, the church featured a gravel parking lot that provided some relief from the mud created by the constant drizzle. During my first few months as pastor of this small church, I had discovered that the congregation had raised enough money to blacktop the parking lot some years before. However, once the money was in hand, a number of bills came due, and the board decided to use the money to pay them off rather than pave the lot. Just enough money remained to gravel the parking lot. Though it was better than nothing, water continued to pool in tire tracks, and many Sundays church members sloshed through puddles.

Fewer than fifteen cars were parked in the lot on a normal Sunday morning. Even with my short tenure, I could tell who was absent from church just by looking at the cars in the lot. A new car signaled visitors, but that did not happen often. Even when visitors came, they never returned.

As I reached into my pocket for the key to the church's main door, I glanced back down the combined church and parsonage driveway. A parklike landscape of tall evergreen trees shadowed the extensive grass lawn that circled the church and parsonage. Wild blackberry bushes grew along the entire west edge of the property. A few fruit trees shaded the north property line, while the street bordered the east and south sides. Less than three blocks away ran one of the major freeways in the city. It was far enough away to mask the traffic noise but close enough to provide good access to the church.

My wife and children loved the two-story parsonage. With nearly three thousand square feet of space, it provided all the room we needed. We lived on the main floor, and our children used the basement as a very large playroom. The fireplace in the spacious living room drove the chill away on rainy evenings. Our third home in four years, it was the nicest one we had lived in up to that time. Every day we counted our blessings, because we certainly could not have afforded to purchase such a spacious home ourselves.

After turning on the lights in the church foyer, I made my way into the hallway near the Sunday school rooms. The church's ample education space had room for nearly one hundred children to participate in Sunday school, along with extra room for youth and adult classes. But only two classes met each Sunday—one for adults and one for children. The children's class had just two children in it—both mine.

As I made my way through the sanctuary, I stopped and prayed at each of the twenty-two beautifully crafted hardwood pews that could seat 220 people. Everything matched—the pulpit, pulpit chairs, pews. It was really very nice. Ten years before I accepted the call to pastor this church, it had reached a peak attendance of around two hundred people. Unfortunately, the church suffered two splits before I arrived, and attendance on Sunday morning now averaged between thirty and thirty-five people. In an effort to create a sense of community during the worship service, all of the people sat on one side of the sanctuary, which was fine until visitors came. It was uncanny, but the visitors always managed to sit on the wrong side, away from

12

the regular worshipers. This left them sitting alone with eleven rows of empty seats around them. This was far from the best welcome a visitor could experience.

When I interviewed for the pastorate of this church, members assured me they wanted their little church to grow. After I arrived, the eleven-member board gave me permission to try just about anything I wanted, but only three members were willing to invest their time and energy toward developing the church's ministry. Most church members simply sat back to watch it all happen. My small team of three interested laypersons made several efforts to reach new people—door-to-door evangelism, a little advertising in the neighborhood, a vacation Bible school, monthly social events—yet nothing we tried seemed to work.

A later attempt to merge with a sister church met with initial optimism but was eventually rejected by the two families who controlled our church. Even a valiant try to relocate the church to a growing part of the community was turned down by church members who could not bear to leave the building where some in their family had been baptized, married, and memorialized with brass name plates on the furniture.

Sitting in my office that rainy day, I finally admitted to myself that I had no idea how to raise the morale or restore a desire for biblical church growth in this congregation. Past experiences in other churches, my top-notch seminary training, even a degree in biblical studies from college gave me few answers. My classes in Greek, Hebrew, church history, Christian education, apologetics, and theology had, of course, provided a seminal foundation for ministry. I soon learned, however, that those disciplines did not help in accomplishing daily tasks, such as assimilating newcomers, dealing with power families, initiating change, building the Sunday school, casting vision, relating to church culture, identifying growth opportunities, engaging in spiritual warfare, understanding the impact a church's location has on its growth, and other similar issues.

The bottom line was that the church was in trouble, and so was I. I knew how to administer an existing Sunday school, but how could I build a Sunday school from scratch? I knew how to motivate passionate church leaders, but how could I revive discouraged leaders?

I knew how to assimilate newcomers in a growing church, but how could I attract people to a dying church?

Discovering Church Growth

In my search for answers to these challenges, I was drawn to the early writings on church growth principles. And as numerous pastors and church leaders have discovered during the past quarter century, I found that church growth principles and strategies provided useful answers to the practical questions I was asking.

I was not surprised to learn that spiritual factors play a major role in the growth of a church. Walk into churches that are experiencing biblical church growth, and you will sense a spiritual passion for finding the lost and involving newcomers. Visit a declining church, and often you will find a selfish attitude (often disguised as fellowship) that results in little concern for Christ's mission to "seek and to save that which was lost" (Luke 19:10). Growing churches always seem to evidence a desire to fulfill the Great Commission, while many declining churches show limited commitment to Christ's command.

As I continued to study church growth principles, I became aware of some practical issues I never would have considered. For example, I learned that many of the problems a church faces are not theological. It had interested me that less than a mile away on the other side of the freeway a church with similar theological convictions as the church I served was going through a season of spiritual and numerical growth. After surveying people living on the other side of the freeway, it became clear that they were unwilling to drive over the freeway to where our church was located. The problem was related to the fact that the church I served was located in an increasingly industrialized area. According to most families at that time, an industrial area was not an appropriate location for a church. No matter how much we went door-to-door or advertised our ministry, people were not going to drive the mile over the freeway to our church.

My study of church growth principles also made me aware of the social dynamics that affect a church's growth. For instance, I discovered that my church had become sealed off from the community, and the driving

14

force of a sealed-off church is not the Great Commission but the desire to protect itself from further hurt. The two splits experienced in the church resulted in the ripping apart of friendships. The hurt from these two unfortunate events caused the leaders to turn inward, refrain from starting new ministries, and resist building friendships with new people. The result was a sealed-off church that was friendly to newcomers on the surface but resistant to the establishment of true friendships.

As I gained more understanding of my church's situation, it became apparent that the congregation was unwilling to cooperate with God in the growth of their church. Even though God was bringing growth to other churches in our community, the congregation I served would not take the necessary steps to get on board with what God was doing. In spite of the congregation's verbal yes to church growth, the members were not willing to pay the price of opening up their fellowship to newcomers. They were not willing to take reasonable risks to establish new ministries. They seemed to think that the mission of their church was to train young preachers for a year or two and send them on their way.

Perhaps it was youthful impatience, but eventually I too left that church. Over the last three decades, I have continued to observe that small church from a distance, and today it remains about the same size. The neighborhood has more homes in it, but still the church cannot reach the people living there. A few years ago the church sold the parsonage. Now a doctor's office stands in its place, reducing the church's property to an even smaller parcel. The parking lot is still gravel, but people do park in the doctor's nice lot next door.

A Major Question

Your church experience may be quite different from the one I described, but I share it because it led me to ask a basic question that nearly all church leaders and participants are asking: *How can we work with God to build a faithful church?*

This question has been the focus of my ministry for nearly thirty years. While pastoring in Southern California in the late 1970s, I studied church growth principles at Fuller Seminary for three years under C. Peter Wagner. Later, in the early 1980s, I worked with Dr. Win Arn at the Institute for American Church Growth. As vice president of consulting services, I was responsible for overseeing consultation with more than five hundred churches, leading training seminars, and conducting church growth analyses of local congregations. The experience of working full-time as a church growth consultant across numerous denominations was invaluable to my understanding of how God builds faithful churches.

In 1986 I accepted an invitation to become professor of Christian ministry and leadership at Talbot School of Theology, Biola University. This position has allowed me time to do research and reflect on the biblical basis for church growth. In 1987 my wife and I founded the McIntosh Church Growth Network consulting ministry, and I continue to do church growth consulting and training events throughout the United States and Canada. To date I have worked with fifty-five denominations or affiliations of churches, led more than two hundred seminars on church growth, and personally analyzed three hundred and eighty-four different churches.

> How can we work with God to build a faithful church?

As I write this book, I am in my twenty-eighth year as a participant, observer, and researcher of the church growth movement in the United States. After all these years and experiences, I have concluded that church growth principles, theology, and theory, *rightly understood,* still provide biblical answers on how to grow a faithful church.

The key words are *rightly understood.* Throughout the years I have listened to and questioned the critics of the church growth movement, and I have come to the conclusion that most people simply misunderstand what church growth is all about. While there are legitimate, thoughtful critics who have taken time to study the biblical principles of church growth, most people have a popular misunderstanding of this concept.

A Popular Misunderstanding

From its very beginning, church growth ideas have been placed under a microscope. The decade of the 1970s was a time of discovery, teaching, debate, adaptation, and clarification of church growth principles in North America. By the 1980s church growth teaching received recognition as a serious discipline dedicated to helping local churches reach their greatest effectiveness in disciple making. Pastors, denominational executives, and laypersons came to understand that church growth was not a "numbers game," as some initially thought, but a purposeful process for winning people to Christ, assimilating them into local churches, and equipping them for ministry.

During the 1990s, a number of subspecializations began to be placed under the broad banner of church growth. These included church planting, cell groups, megachurch models, prayer, spiritual warfare, generational studies, conflict management, change agency, long-range planning, and fund-raising. While some of these areas of ministry are compatible to a lesser or greater degree with church growth principles and theory, they represent a subtle shift away from a clear focus on the foundational biblical principles of church growth. The conceptual broadening of church growth to embrace more and more of these subspecializations of ministry created, to a large extent, a popular misunderstanding and ambiguity about the movement.

While some church leaders understand that the primary focus of church growth is the fulfillment of the Great Commission (Matt. 28:19–20), a common perception is that church growth is all about techniques, methods, and models. For example, two well-known authors have expressed this perception—Charles Colson and Jim Cymbala. Both of these men are godly leaders, but they define church growth solely in popular terms. For example, writing in his book *The Body,* Charles Colson comments, "Church growth has become the hottest business in the religious world today. If 'the customer is king,' then the church has to react as any organization does to consumer demand, which means finding the right *marketing strategy*."[1] Taking a different slant, Jim Cymbala declares in *Fresh Wind, Fresh Fire,* "Instead of trying to bring men and women to Christ in the biblical way, we are consumed with the unbiblical concept of 'church growth.'"[2] He believes that church growth is just a methodology used to finesse people into a church to increase its numbers.

Colson and Cymbala mean well, and it's lamentable that they have misunderstood and misrepresented the true nature of church growth. They and other sincere critics are perpetuating a popular perception of the movement rather than seeking to understand its core biblical principles. This has happened in part due to the fact that the term *church growth* has been broadened to include meanings and ideas that it never was intended to imply.

Originally the term *church growth* was coined to reference the results that could be expected from faithful disciple making. A congregation that wins people to Christ, assimilates the new converts into the local body, and then teaches them all that Christ commanded can expect to see church growth—numerical and spiritual.

Basically *church growth* means "all that is involved in bringing men and women who do not have a personal relationship to Jesus Christ into fellowship with Him and into responsible church membership."[3] Most of us would not quarrel with the concept of church growth when it is defined in this way. It is what the early church experienced when "those who had received his word were baptized" and about three thousand souls were added to the church (Acts 2:41). We all desire that people be brought to Christ and into local churches where they can be discipled. But as Ralph Winter, founder of the U.S. Center for World Mission, suggested some time ago, "Like many other things, the phrase 'church growth' can be hijacked and flown to unintended destinations."[4] Clearly, this has happened.

An example of what has taken place with the term *church growth* can be illustrated by what happened to the names *Kleenex* and *Xerox*. Kleenex and Xerox are brand names of a particular brand facial tissue and photocopier. Both words, however, have been popularized (hijacked) to mean all tissues and all photocopiers. Today one draws a Kleenex out of a Scotties box of tissues and makes a Xerox on a Canon copier. In a similar way, many approaches to church ministry are labeled "church growth" even though they do not fit into the original understanding of the term. Thus my goal in this book is to return to the more biblical concept of church growth.

Becoming a Faithful Church

At a number of my conferences, I have asked pastors and church leaders to answer three questions: Do you want your church to decline?

18

Do you want your church to plateau? Do you want your church to grow? As you might guess, they all have said they want their churches to grow. In fact I have never had even one person indicate he wanted his church to decline or plateau.

Imagine asking Jesus these three questions. What do you think he would say? Well, he has already answered by declaring, "I will build My church; and the gates of Hades will not overpower it" (Matt. 16:18). Jesus Christ did not suffer and die on Calvary to build a powerless, declining church. Rather, he sovereignly promises that his church will grow. We all want our churches to experience growth—biblical growth! As we obediently cooperate with God's life-giving principles for growth, it can happen. There is hope for your church!

That is what this book is all about—learning to cooperate with God in building a faithful church. What is a faithful church? A faithful church is one that is loyal to God and his work in the world. A church's source of faithfulness arises out of the very nature of God himself. Moses declared, "The Rock! His work is perfect, for all His ways are just; a God of faithfulness and without injustice, righteous and upright is He" (Deut. 32:4). The psalmist comments, "Your lovingkindness, O LORD, extends to the heavens, your faithfulness reaches to the skies" (Ps. 36:5). Our faithful God is trustworthy, loyal, and reliable. We can trust him because he is totally dependable. It is his nature to be faithful.

God's faithfulness to his people is unconditional, but he desires a reciprocal loyalty in our relationship to him. Christ, the head of the church, modeled faithfulness through obedience to his Father. "He was faithful to Him who appointed Him, as Moses also was in all His house. . . . Christ was faithful as a Son over His house—whose house we are" (Heb. 3:2, 6). Thus it is no surprise that Paul writes, "Moreover it is required in stewards, that a man be found faithful" (1 Cor. 4:2 KJV). Since Christ is head of the church, his body must reflect his faithful nature.

The core element of faithfulness is obedience to God's commands. As the psalmist notes: "I have chosen the faithful way; I have placed Your ordinances before me" (Ps. 119:30). Jesus put it clearly: "Why do you call Me, 'Lord, Lord,' and do not do what I say?" (Luke 6:46).

A church's program, budget, worship attendance, or any of a host of other aspects is not the prime indicator of its faithfulness. The prime indicator is a church's obedience to God's commands and purpose in the world. While it is possible for a church to be faithful and not experience numerical growth, such a church should still demonstrate a strong desire for such growth. For example, obedience to God's purpose in the world might be seen through the church's effort to reach the people in its area of influence through church planting efforts, either in cooperation with its denominational affiliation or alone. A church that cannot exhibit clear obedience to God's plan in the world could rightfully be labeled unfaithful, no matter how effective its ministries appear on the surface. Of course, a church that grows numerically might also be an unfaithful church if it is not also working to extend God's work in the world. An example might be seen in a church that grows purely via transfers from other churches but puts forth no real effort to win new converts to Christ.

For the most part, churches that seek to follow obediently God's command and purpose in the world will experience at least a measure of numerical growth. Simply put, your church will experience biblical church growth when it obediently cooperates with God's life-giving principles. By using the term *biblical* to describe church growth, I simply mean growth that is achieved according to God's principles as found in his Word.

Biblical church growth is a journey, not a destination. I invite you to journey with me as we look at biblical church growth principles. In our journey together we will explore several questions all leaders need to ask and answer about the churches they serve:

What is God's purpose in church growth?
What is our authority for church growth?
What is our ultimate goal in church growth?
What are our procedures for church growth?
What is our power for church growth?
What is the duty of our leaders in church growth?
What is the role of our people in church growth?
What is our approach to church growth?
What is our plan for church growth?

What is our locale for church growth?

What is our structure for church growth?

What is holding us back from church growth?

My prayer is that *Biblical Church Growth* will be the beginning of a journey that will result in your church cooperating with God in building a faithful church.

Grant us, good Lord, wisdom to understand our duty and courage to do it, counting no labor too great. In Christ's blessed name we ask. Amen.

Donald A. McGavran[5]

Questions to Ask and Answer

1. When you think of church growth, what ideas or concepts come to mind?
2. What criticisms of church growth have you read or heard? Do you agree or disagree with them?
3. Do you agree with the original concept of church growth as faithful disciple making? Why or why not?
4. How would you define a faithful church and how does your definition contrast with the ideas presented in this chapter?
5. Is it possible for a church to be faithful if it does not experience numerical growth or spiritual growth? Why or why not?

TWO

The Life-Giving Church

There is an inescapable theological bearing to the matter. The Church and its mission are not man's creation. They are rooted in God.

Donald A. McGavran

You may have never thought of it, but every day we solve complicated physics problems in practice. For instance, if you play tennis, you must gauge the speed and angle of the ball heading your way. In a split second you adjust the angle of your racquet and calculate how much speed and force to apply to return the ball and keep it in bounds. While figuring all that out, you also gauge a wide list of variables, such as the speed and direction of the wind and the time needed to get to the ball before it bounces twice on your side of the net. The entire process involves a great deal of difficult problem solving, but you do it in a split second.

Most of us could not begin to solve such physics problems on paper. If we tried to apply numbers to all the variables created while playing tennis, it would be nearly impossible to figure out. Even with super computers to aid us, very few people would know how to begin the calculations. Fewer would come up with the correct answers.

No matter what we do, it is almost always easier to know *how* to do something than to know *why* something works. Consider everything from cooking to building. Many grandmothers are fantastic cooks, but most find it difficult to explain why their cooking is so delicious. If they give you their secret recipe, the dish is rarely as good when you make it. The same is true when erecting a building. A number of people know how to lay brick, frame a wall, or run electric lines. Yet few know why it all comes together to create a well-built building. That's the reason the architect is paid more than the bricklayer. The architect has more extensive knowledge and understands the why.

Likewise, it is easier to know *how* to grow a church than *why* a church grows. Ask laypeople in a growing church *why* their church is thriving, and you will get a number of illustrations of *how.* The usual answers include, "We are praying more." "Our people are hard workers." "The pastor is an excellent communicator." Pastors are usually no better at answering the same question. Some point to a new youth pastor, others to the addition of a second worship service, still others to a relocation effort. Each of the programs or people mentioned certainly fits into the overall growth mix, but none of the respondents delves into the deeper issue of *why* the church is growing. The pastor or layperson who knows how to start a small-group ministry, lead a worship service, or teach is valuable. But like the architect, the individual who knows *why* it all works together to create growth possesses valuable knowledge.

The Alligator Factor

In practice, people are actually more concerned about the *how* than the *why.* Seminars, workshops, and classes are offered every year to train people in the how-tos of ministry. They have such titles as:

How to Assimilate Newcomers into Your Church
How to Attract and Welcome Visitors
How to Mobilize Your Laity
Bringing Clarity to Your Preaching

Leading and Managing Your Church
Reaching Baby Boomers
Developing Self-Motivated Teams

Each of the seminars listed above focuses on the *doing* of ministry rather than the *being* of ministry—the *how* rather than the *why*. The interest of people in learning the *how* of ministry is driven by the pressures of life. A familiar sign posted in coffee rooms in many businesses says it well: "It's difficult to remember that your objective is to drain the swamp when the alligators are biting." For people involved in day-to-day ministry, the alligators are biting, and they want practical answers on how to do ministry more effectively. It is not that the *why* is unimportant; it just does not seem as urgent.

A few years ago a friend of mine led a national seminar called "How to Reach Baby Boomers." Attendance ran in the hundreds as people came out to learn how to reach North America's largest generation. A few years later my friend offered another national seminar called "Spiritual Factors of Church Growth," and so few people responded that the seminar was canceled. The reason? People assumed they knew and understood the *why* (spiritual factors), but the pressing need was to learn *how* to reach a particular generation (alligator factor).

It is frequently true that people who say church growth does not work have attempted some of the *hows* without giving serious thought to the *whys*. I call this the seminar syndrome. The seminar syndrome materializes when church leaders attend the conference sponsored by a well-known church, receive a basic overview of how the church developed, and then return to their own churches to put their newfound ideas into practice. More often than not the attempts to repeat the new methodology in their churches fail. They then say, "Church growth doesn't work."

The problem is that they did not apply church growth principles (the *whys*) but focused on a particular approach (the *hows*). Knowing and using methods is fine, but when the user doesn't understand the essential *whys* behind the methods, he or she is in danger of failing. Faithful churches become effective not simply because they do the right things (*hows*) but because they understand why the right things

24

need to be done. Unfortunately, what we catch from a seminar, workshop, or conference are usually the *hows* rather than the *whys*.

Noted church growth authority Elmer Towns is fond of saying, "Methods are many; principles are few. Methods never last; principles always do." *Biblical Church Growth* is a book of *whys* more than *hows*.

This means I am going to focus on principles of church growth and their biblical foundations more than on methodologies, techniques, or strategies, because methodologies, techniques, and strategies are culturally derived and thus have limited life spans. For example, in the mid-1970s it was quite popular for a church to have a bus ministry. Several megachurches of that era had found that people were receptive to being picked up at their homes and brought to church on buses. As the word spread that this new methodology was helpful in winning new converts to Christ, many churches purchased buses and began to transport people to church.

> Faithful churches become effective not simply because they do the right things *(hows)* but because they understand why the right things need to be done.

Today very few churches use bus ministries for outreach. It's not that the principle of finding and reaching receptive people for Christ has changed; for most churches, the methodology has changed. If a church experiences growth due to a particular approach to ministry, its growth is limited to the lifetime of the method. However, if a church builds on unchanging principles, the potential for growth is ongoing.

If you picked up this book looking for the latest church growth strategy, methodology, or technique, you will not find it. But do not despair. If you carefully work through the book chapter by chapter, you will come to discern the life-giving principles behind the methods. Better yet, you will be able to design your own unique approaches, perfectly fitted to your own church.

The Life-Giving God

The central question is not *How do churches grow?* but rather *Why should churches grow?* The answer to the first question varies, which I will address later. The answer to the second question is found in the nature of God.

God is a life-giving God, and it is his very nature to give life to whatever he does. The very first statement in the Bible about God is familiar: "In the beginning God created the heavens and the earth" (Gen. 1:1). The Bible begins with the declaration that there was a beginning to the world and that God was already there. In existence from all eternity, God is life, and thus he is the only one who can give life to others.

The life-giving nature of God is demonstrated in the acts of creation. God first established an environment to sustain life by creating the heavens, earth, light, and water necessary for creation to live (vv. 2–10). Once the proper environment was established, God created plant life, aquatic life, and animal life (vv. 11–25).

The crowning achievement of God's work came on the sixth day. "Then the LORD God formed man of dust from the ground" (2:7). God "formed" or "molded" man personally. On the previous days God simply said, "Let there be . . ." and it was done. Bringing life to humankind was more intimate, involving God's personal touch. Imagine a potter carefully molding a clay pot with his personal touch (see Jer. 18:2–6). God took great care by molding man, as it were, with his own hands. The reason God took such great care in forming man was that "God created man in His own image, in the image of God He created him; male and female He created them" (Gen. 1:27). Humankind is at once lowly and dignified, formed from the dust of the ground in the image of God, by his personal touch.

God's personal involvement in the forming of humankind was even more intimate in that he "breathed into his nostrils the breath of life; and man became a living being" (2:7). God formed the body of man, but it was lifeless until God energized it with his own breath. Life can come only from life, and the life-giving God is the only self-existent being. Thus God was able to impart life to humankind. King David expressed awe and wonder when he thought of God and of humankind's place in creation. He wrote in Psalm 8:

> When I consider Your heavens, the work of Your fingers,
> The moon and the stars, which You have ordained;

What is man that You take thought of him,
And the son of man that You care for him?
Yet You have made him a little lower than God,
And You crown him with glory and majesty!
You make him to rule over the works of Your hands;
You have put all things under his feet,
All sheep and oxen,
And also the beasts of the field,
The birds of the heavens and the fish of the sea,
Whatever passes through the paths of the seas.

verses 3–8

The "breath of the spirit of life" is also shared by animals (Gen. 7:22). However, it was only to man that God directly breathed the breath of life. Humankind is the crown of God's creation, a higher order than animals, in part due to the direct empowerment of life from the life-giving God.

The last act of God's creative work was the fashioning of woman. All of the animals had been made both male and female and were instructed to multiply (1:22, 24). Only Adam was alone, a fact he soon discovered while naming the animals that came to him (2:20). So the Lord fashioned a unique helper for the man from out of his life. God used the life (bone and flesh) from the man's living body to make the woman. Thus both the man and the woman experienced God's intimate touch in their creation. When God brought the woman to man, he immediately recognized that she was part of his life. He exclaimed, "This is now bone of my bones, and flesh of my flesh; she shall be called Woman, because she was taken out of Man" (v. 23).

Adam and Eve's most basic experience of God was that he loved them and provided for their care. God planted a delightful garden in Eden. In it were beautiful trees that were good for food (Gen. 2:8–9). He initially placed Adam, later Eve, in the garden, which undoubtedly provided for all their physical, emotional, and spiritual needs.

Morally free beings "in his own image" must be allowed to respond to God of their own free will, so Adam and Eve were free to return God's love or not to love God. God had given them life, a beautiful home, abundant food, purpose in living, literally everything they needed. Now it was their choice to love him in return.

God gave Adam, and ultimately Eve, a command to be obeyed. First, God called their attention to his abundant provision: "From any tree of the garden you may eat freely" (v. 16). There was such an abundant variety of foods that Adam and Eve's hunger always would have been fully satisfied. Then God placed one restraint on them: "From the tree of the knowledge of good and evil you shall not eat" (v. 17a). It was a simple command that would have been easy for Adam and Eve to obey. Would they obey the one who had shown such love to them, or would they disobey his word and turn to their own ways? Finally, God warned them of the consequences for disobedience: "For in the day that you eat from it you will surely die" (v. 17b). True life is available only through communion and connection with the life-giving God. The opposite of life is death, or separation from the life-giving God. Therefore the primary warning was related to spiritual death (separation from God) but also to physical death, because God is the source of both spiritual and physical life. Literally, God's warning was, "Dying, you shall die." If Adam and Eve disobeyed God, they would experience spiritual death immediately and physical death ultimately.

Since Adam and Eve were innocent, with an untested righteousness, there was nothing within their nature to lead them to disobey God. They would have to be persuaded by something outside of themselves to make a personal, moral choice to disobey. Through a process of deception and blatant denial, the serpent (identified as Satan in Rev. 12:9) created a situation in which Adam and Eve chose to disobey God's command (Gen. 3:1–7). Apparently Eve was deceived, but Adam chose willfully to disobey God (1 Tim. 2:14), and it was through him that "sin entered into the world, and death through sin, and so death spread to all men, because all sinned" (Rom. 5:12).

Shortly after Adam and Eve disobeyed, God came looking for them in the garden. They had become acutely aware of their sin and attempted to cover their guilt by making clothes for themselves from plant leaves. Deep in their conscience they knew such coverings were useless, and so they attempted to hide.

God, of course, already realized what Adam and Eve had done (Gen. 3:11), but his life-giving nature caused him to search for and find his lost children. "Where are you?" he asked (v. 9), a question that prompted Adam to admit his guilt and fear (v. 10). After a series of vain attempts to blame others, Adam, Eve, and the serpent received God's judgment for their disobedience (vv. 14–19). True to God's warning, the man and woman lost fellowship with God as he drove them out of the garden (v. 24), and eventually they experienced physical death (5:5).

As a result of the sin and rebellion of Adam and Eve, spiritual and physical death spread to all people, but not without the hope of salvation, as the apostle Paul explained in Romans 5. "Therefore, just as through one man sin entered into the world, and death through sin . . . even so through the obedience of the One the many will be made righteous . . . to eternal life through Jesus Christ our Lord" (vv. 12, 19, 21). Within his righteous judgments, God gave two hints that he would graciously provide a way for Adam and Eve, as well as their children, to regain fellowship with him. One indication is that he clothed them with garments made of skin (Gen. 3:21), because the coverings they had made were totally inadequate. It took the shedding of innocent blood to provide a proper covering for them (this prefigures the atonement; see Lev. 17:11). The second indication is that he promised a coming Redeemer.

Genesis 3:15 has long been called the "first gospel" (*Protevangelium*). In the judgment pronounced on the serpent, God promised, "I will put enmity between you and the woman, and between your seed and her seed; He shall bruise you on the head, and you shall bruise him on the heel." In general this judgment indicates a continued battle between good and evil, as illustrated shortly thereafter between Cain and Abel (4:1–8). Specifically, however, it refers to the coming of a Person who would win the ultimate victory over the devil. This Person was, of course, Jesus Christ, who was crushed for our iniquities when he died on the cross (Isa. 53:5). At first his death appeared to be a mortal wound, but he rose from the grave the third day, winning the victory over the serpent (see Heb. 2:14; Rev. 20:10).

God's promised blessing to Abram, "In you all the families of the earth will be blessed" (Gen. 12:3), was to come through Jesus Christ.

His purpose was to be a life-giving Savior: "For as in Adam all die, so also in Christ all will be made alive" (1 Cor. 15:22).

The Life-Giving Savior

The life-giving story of God continues in the New Testament. No other book in the Bible demonstrates the life-giving nature of Jesus Christ as carefully as does the Gospel of John. Looking back to creation, the apostle John mirrors the words of Genesis in the opening statement of his Gospel: "In the beginning was the Word, and the Word was with God, and the Word was God. He was in the beginning with God. All things came into being through Him, and apart from Him nothing came into being that has come into being. *In Him was life* and the life was the Light of men. The Light shines in the darkness, and the darkness did not comprehend it" (John 1:1–5, italics mine).

John carefully intermingled words from Genesis 1, such as *life, light,* and *darkness,* to show that his theme had roots in the beginning of creation. The "Word" is Christ, as John later directly states, "He is clothed with a robe dipped in blood, and His name is called The Word of God" (Rev. 19:13; see also John 1:14).

All three persons of the Godhead were involved in the creation. The Father created, but he did it through the Holy Spirit (Gen. 1:2) and the Son (1 Cor. 8:6). However, Jesus Christ had a unique role, as described in Colossians 1:16–17: "For by Him all things were created, both in the heavens and on earth, visible and invisible, whether thrones or dominions or rulers or authorities—all things have been created through Him and for Him. He is before all things, and in Him all things hold together."

More important than creating the world, according to John, is the fact that Jesus is the life-giver. "In Him was life," John declares. The source of life is in the Father, but He gave to the Son to have life in Himself. John discloses, "For just as the Father has life in Himself, even so He gave to the Son also to have life in Himself" (John 5:26; see also 1 John 5:11–12).

Indeed, John says that the purpose in writing his Gospel is "that you may believe that Jesus is the Christ, the Son of God; and that *believing you may have life in His name*" (John 20:31, italics mine). True to his purpose, John builds the case for Jesus Christ being a life-giving Savior throughout his Gospel. God gave his only Son, "that whoever believes in Him shall not perish, but have eternal life" (3:16). Only those who believe in the Son will have life, and those who do not believe will not see life (v. 36). Jesus asserts that he is the "bread of life," and whoever eats of this bread shall live forever (6:35–51). Prior to raising Lazarus, Jesus claims, "I am the resurrection and the life; he who believes in Me will live even if he dies, and everyone who lives and believes in Me will never die" (11:25–26).

Jesus gives and sustains physical life (see Col. 1:16), but his primary purpose in coming to earth was to provide eternal life. Nothing confirms this more than his own words: "I came that they may have life, and have it abundantly" (John 10:10). The apostle Paul writes, "For the wages of sin is death, but the free gift of God is eternal life in Christ Jesus our Lord" (Rom. 6:23).

In a strange paradox, Jesus Christ, who embodies life itself, had to experience death on a cross so that he could provide life to humankind. John the apostle instructs Christ's followers: "He Himself is the propitiation [satisfaction] for our sins; and not for ours only, but also for those of the whole world" (1 John 2:2). The justice of God had to be satisfied, and to do so required a sinless sacrifice. It was necessary for Christ to become like one of us (John 1:14), live a sinless life (Heb. 4:15), and "taste death for everyone" (Heb. 2:9) to provide eternal life for all who believe in him. This is the essence of the gospel message that must be believed to have eternal spiritual life. As Paul carefully explains: "Now I make known to you, brethren, the gospel which I preached to you, which also you received, in which also you stand, by which also you are saved, . . . that Christ died for our sins according to the Scriptures, and that He was buried, and that He was raised on the third day according to the Scriptures, and that He appeared to Cephas, then to the twelve" (1 Cor. 15:1–5).

Life comes from believing that Christ died for our sins (proved by his burial) and that he rose from the grave (proved by his being seen by many). There is no other way to receive life. Jesus is the only mediator between humankind and God (1 Tim. 2:5–6), a fact that Jesus boldly announced: "I am the way, and the truth, and the life; no one comes to the Father but through Me" (John 14:6).

As the life-giving Savior, Jesus continues to seek and save the lost (Luke 19:10; see also Mark 1:38), just as God did with Adam and Eve following their rebellion. This is his purpose in coming to earth. Those who believe in him and receive new life are "born again" (John 3:3) and become new creations (2 Cor. 5:17). They become part of the life-giving church of which he is the head (Col. 1:18).

The Life-Giving Church

In the very first mention of his church, Jesus sovereignly guarantees its growth: "I will build my church" (Matt. 16:18). How could he make such a claim? As the life-giving Savior, he is head of the church. His nature is to give life, and the church, his body, is responsible to share that life with the world.

A church (Greek *ekklesia*) is an assembly of people. In the New Testament the word is used in reference to an assembly of Christians, with both a universal and a local connotation. The universal church is a spiritual body composed of all people who have professed faith in Jesus Christ alone for salvation (see Eph. 1:22–23). A local church is an assembly of baptized Christians who have organized themselves to fulfill the Great Commission in a particular geographical area, as well as to carry out other responsibilities given to it (see 1 Cor. 1:2; 1 Thess. 1:1).[1] When Christ proclaimed that he would build his church, both the universal church and local churches were included in seed form. Growth of the universal church takes place primarily as local churches faithfully win people to Christ and assimilate the new converts into their body. Christ is, of course, the head over both the universal and local dimensions of his church.

Christ's headship over the church is a natural outcome of his life-giving nature that began in creation and continues in his role as Savior of the body. "For by Him," Paul writes, "all things were created, both in the heavens and on earth . . . all things have been created through Him and for Him. He is also head of the body, the church" (Col. 1:16, 18). "And He put all things in subjection under His feet, and gave Him as head over all things to the church, which is His body, the fullness of Him who fills all in all" (Eph. 1:22–23). "For the husband is the head of the wife, as Christ also is the head of the church, He Himself being the Savior of the body" (5:23).

As an expression of Christ's living body, the local church is to be a channel of life for both spiritual birth and spiritual growth. The early church experienced such balanced growth. Observe the natural interplay of spiritual birth and spiritual growth in Acts 2:41–42: "So then, those who had received his word were baptized; and that day there were added about three thousand souls [spiritual birth]. They were continually devoting themselves to the apostles' teaching and to fellowship, to the breaking of bread and to prayer [spiritual growth]."

The body must do what its head directs. Thus Paul encourages Christ's church to focus on spiritual birth and spiritual growth. "Let the word of Christ richly dwell within you," Paul encourages, "with all wisdom teaching and admonishing one another with psalms and hymns and spiritual songs, singing with thankfulness in your hearts to God" (Col. 3:16). Then in the following chapter he admonishes the church to keep focusing outward: "Conduct yourselves with wisdom toward outsiders, making the most of the opportunity. Let your speech always be with grace, as though seasoned with salt, so that you will know how you should respond to each person" (4:5–6).

Spiritual growth of the body is crucial, but it is also to be expected that a church will grow numerically as spiritual births are added to the church fellowship. "There were added about three thousand souls," Luke writes (Acts 2:41). Added to what? They were added to the church in Jerusalem. Using a different picture, the apostle Peter reminds young believers that Christ is the living stone (see Ps. 118:22; Eph. 2:20), and they are each smaller living stones being built up into a spiritual house (1 Peter 2:4–5). The image is of a house that is not finished. The builder is still in the process of adding new stones to the building through the testimony of those who are already part of it (v. 9). As each new stone is added, it takes its place in the building and brings glory to the builder. Each stone is taken from darkness and placed in the light, where it can be seen by those not yet a part of the building as a witness to the builder's excellence (vv. 6–12).

33

Jesus is the living Savior. He is head over a living body, his church. Is it possible that he is head over a dead church, a declining church, a stagnant church? In the universal picture of the church, the answer is no. He is a life-giving Savior, and the church, his body, must therefore be a life-giving church. His sovereign promise that his church will grow still holds true. Unfortunately, in reality, the local church is often dead, declining, or stagnant. This should not be the norm, however. Every church should demonstrate the vitality of its head, Jesus Christ.

> Jesus is a life-giving Savior, and the church, his body, must therefore be a life-giving church.

The promise and imperative of church growth explodes from the heart of God. The life-giving Father is concerned with giving new life to humankind through the salvation that comes, at great cost, only through his life-giving Son. He sent his Son into the world that "the world might be saved through Him" (John 3:17), and his desire is for none to perish "but for all to come to repentance" (2 Peter 3:9). We cannot escape the fact that the church and its life-giving mission are God's creation; therefore, biblical church growth is rooted in the life-giving nature of the Godhead. As the expression of Christ's church in our local setting, we are not free to select what end or purpose we will follow.

Why do some churches grow? The answer is complex, but, simply put, churches grow as they cooperate with God in bringing life to a lost world. Just as Adam and Eve were free to choose to obey or disobey God, so individual churches are free to choose to cooperate or not cooperate with God in bringing life to a lost world.

How can we cooperate with God in building a faithful church? This can be accomplished by following the life-giving principles of biblical church growth. In the chapters that follow I will describe these nine principles.

Almighty God, ruler of the nations, You have declared, "I am God and there is no other." You created the world and all tribes and classes

of mankind. And then, good Lord, You sent Your Son Jesus Christ our Lord to reveal Your will for mankind and to become the one suffi-cient sacrifice for sin. You call all men to repentance and to salvation through faith in His mighty name. Only by confessing Him as Sav-ior and Lord may men be saved. Bring speedily, O God, that day when sin and death will be overcome, when the new heavens and the new earth will be inaugurated, and Your will will be done on earth as it is in heaven. In Christ's name we pray. Amen.

Donald A. McGavran[2]

Questions to Ask and Answer

1. Who is the source of biblical church growth and how should this fact impact our churches?
2. What are the implications of the fact that the life-giving Savior is the head of the church? Your church?
3. How does your church demonstrate the life-giving nature of God flowing through it?
4. Why does the life-giving nature of God demand church growth?
5. When did your church most recently try to "seek and save the lost"?

THREE

The Right Premise

God's Word

> We have Jesus Christ our Lord. We have no one else. We have the Bible.
> We have nothing else. In the light of revelation we can go fearlessly forward.
>
> Donald A. McGavran

On one of my consulting trips to New Jersey, I was invited to speak at a church on the subject of biblical church growth. A storm had covered the streets with snow the evening before, which delayed my arrival at the church on Sunday morning. With little time to observe the congregation, I was quickly ushered to the platform just as I was being introduced. Gathering my thoughts, I stepped into the pulpit and began by saying, "Good morning! Please take your Bibles and turn to . . ." Hearing no pages turning, I looked up from my reading to discover that not one person in the congregation had a Bible with him or her. Peeking at the pastor, who was sitting on the platform to my left, I saw that even he did not have a Bible. Quickly sensing the embarrassment of the congregation in response to my instruction, I continued, "If you don't have your Bibles with you today, please listen as I read the passage."

I recognize that today there is a great variety of church worship styles, and I do not mean that carrying a Bible to church is the singular test of one's commitment to the Bible, although it may at times be an indicator of such commitment. As I preached that day, however, I kept thinking how ironic it was that I had been asked to speak about *biblical* church growth to people who did not use their Bibles.

Observation of growing and declining churches over the last three decades, as well as various research studies, suggests that the weaker a church's position is regarding the authority of Scripture, the less likely it is to experience biblical church growth, as illustrated below.[1]

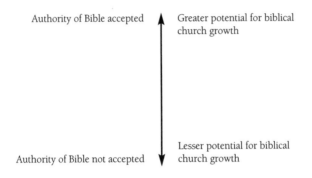

A quick perusal of churches and denominations over the last half century reveals that some used to hold a high view of biblical authority but now allow tradition and/or human reason to stand in judgment over the Bible. It's not surprising that a majority of such churches are mired in church decline, due in part to the lack of an authoritative source for church growth.

Know What You Believe

Biblical church growth begins with the right premise—the Word of God. Simply stated, *life-giving churches have a strong commitment to the authority of God's Word.*

The ultimate source of our authority, of course, is the life-giving God. As the self-existent One, he is not dependent on anything or anyone outside himself. No one existed before him, and he is the high-

The Right Premise—The Word of God

Life-giving churches have a strong commitment
to the authority of God's Word.

est being. God, therefore, has the right, because of who he is and what he has done, to set the standard for belief and practice. He is our authority.

Since he is the life-giving Creator, he alone is the source of all knowledge and truth. However, due to the fact that he is infinite and humankind is finite, we could never know him unless he chose to reveal himself and his desires to us. Fortunately, God has chosen to reveal himself to us in two ways—general revelation and special revelation.

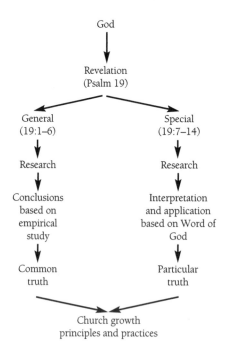

Through general revelation God communicates his truth in nature, history, and human life. The psalmist writes that nature reveals much

about God. "The heavens are telling of the glory of God; and their expanse is declaring the work of His hands" (Ps. 19:1). God also declares his ways through history. The apostle Paul, in his sermon on Mars Hill, speaks of God's revelation in the history of nations. Note how Paul integrates creation, the life-giving nature of God, and his historical work among the nations together in the following passage from Acts (see also Rom. 13:1).

> The God who made the world and all things in it, since He is Lord of heaven and earth, does not dwell in temples made with hands; nor is He served by human hands, as though He needed anything, since He Himself gives to all people life and breath and all things; and He made from one man every nation of mankind to live on all the face of the earth, having determined their appointed times and the boundaries of their habitation.
>
> Acts 17:24–26

Although it is marred by sin, human life also reveals God. Paul reminds us, "For when Gentiles who do not have the Law do instinctively the things of the Law, these, not having the Law, are a law to themselves, in that they show the work of the Law written in their hearts" (Rom. 2:14–15). In a unique way human development, consciousness, and relationships reveal the nature of God.

Knowledge gained through general revelation is God's truth. It is true because it is sourced in the life-giving God. As such, it is biblical to make full use of empirical research in the fields of anthropology, sociology, and other sciences. Why? Because God's general revelation reflects his character; it is intelligible, coherent, and discoverable. Truth discovered from the natural realm of creation, human development, and history is God's truth held in common with all people—believing and nonbelieving. We are free to explore, discover, and use common truths.

As a caution, it is important to point out that study in the many fields of general revelation is a supplement to, not a substitute for, the special revelation of God's Word. Human understanding has been warped due to sin. General revelation is now under a curse (Gen. 3:17–19) and is subject to futility (Rom. 8:20). More critical is the fact

---

The Bottom Line

The Bible is the inspired, authoritative, infallible rule of faith and practice. It is God's Word written. It proclaims that there is general revelation, which God gives to all men as he desires in every age and every culture. God has also given special revelation in Jesus Christ his Son, our Savior, and in the Bible. All general revelation, inevitably mixed with the erroneous ideas of mere men, must be weighed and measured before special revelation. Everything not in accord with special revelation is either only partially true or completely false.

Donald McGavran and Win Arn[2]

---

that sin has left humankind blind and in much darkness when it comes to understanding general revelation. "For even though they knew God, they did not honor Him as God or give thanks, but they became futile in their speculations, and their foolish heart was darkened" (1:21). Satan has actually "blinded the minds of the unbelieving" (2 Cor. 4:4), and such blindness no doubt affects the believer's grasp of general revelation to some extent. Such twisting of our understanding of general revelation seems to impact hard matters such as physics, statistics, and demographics, as well as soft matters such as relationships, sociology, and anthropology. Research into general revelation is appropriate, since it is God's truth, but must always be held in judgment under the objective truth of God's Word. Study of the natural and social sciences must be done with reverence and humility, resulting in modest and tentative pronouncements.

General revelation provides all people with a basic knowledge of God's existence, love, and glory. While each person's recognition of God in nature, history, and humanity may be unconscious, it is there. All will be held accountable because of it (see Rom. 2:11–16). Yet a fuller knowledge of God and his ways is needed beyond that provided by general revelation. There is much more to know about God than can be found by studying nature, history, and humanity. *Revelation* refers specifically to uncovering something that is covered (Greek *apokalypto*), and through special revelation God reveals more of himself and his truth.

Through special revelation God discloses certain things about himself and his truth that we could not discover on our own. The psalmist writes of God's Word, "The law of the LORD is perfect, restoring the soul; the testimony of the LORD is sure, making wise the simple. The precepts of the LORD are right, rejoicing the heart; the commandment of the LORD is pure, enlightening the eyes" (Ps. 19:7–8). Throughout history God has made himself known in special ways at special times to special peoples. For example, God has occasionally revealed himself through miracles, such as when Moses' rod turned into a serpent, which was done "that they may believe that the LORD, the God of their fathers, the God of Abraham, the God of Isaac, and the God of Jacob, has appeared to you" (Exod. 4:5). God has also made himself known through prophecy. Much of what we know of Christ was first revealed through prophecy, such as the virgin birth (Isa. 7:14) and Christ's resurrection (Ps. 16:8–11). However, while miracles and prophecy are important, the two primary modes of special revelation are the revelation of God in Jesus Christ and the revelation of God in the Bible.

The apostle John begins his Gospel with a clear statement of the special revelation of Jesus Christ. He writes, "And the Word became flesh, and dwelt among us, and we saw His glory, glory as of the only begotten from the Father, full of grace and truth" (John 1:14). In a similar fashion the Book of Hebrews begins, "God, after He spoke long ago to the fathers in the prophets in many portions and in many ways, in these last days has spoken to us in His Son, whom He appointed heir of all things, through whom also He made the world" (Heb. 1:1–2). It is in Jesus Christ that we know the Father. "No one has seen God at any time; the only begotten God who is in the bosom of the Father, He has explained Him" (John 1:18). Jesus declared, "He who has seen Me has seen the Father" (14:9). In a special way, Christ reveals more of God's existence, nature, and will than we could ever know through general revelation. Truly, to follow Christ is to follow the Father. "My sheep hear My voice, and I know them, and they follow Me. . . . I and the Father are One" (10:27, 30).

41

To be known and followed, God's authority has to be communicated to humankind. What we know of God from miracles, prophecy, and our Lord Jesus Christ is embodied in an authoritative source. In his wisdom God has chosen to convey his authority to us in a book—the Bible. The Bible is the inspired Word of God, and whatever the Bible says, God says, because God himself "breathed" the words of Scripture (2 Tim. 3:16). The word *inspired (theopneustos)* refers to breath that is exhaled (expired) rather than inhaled. The concept is that the Bible is literally God's exhaled breath, hence, his very words. The idea of God breathing his Word reverberates back to creation when God said, "Let there be . . ." and it was so, and he breathed life into humankind. In a similar manner Scripture was brought into existence by the very breath of God. Thus it is a life-giving Word just as God is a life-giving God.

Since the Bible is God's Word, it naturally follows that the Bible has authority over individual believers and churches. Written over thousands of years by many writers, it is uniquely his Word, for God "spoke long ago to the fathers in the prophets in many portions and in many ways" (Heb. 1:1) as "men moved by the Holy Spirit spoke from God" (2 Peter 1:21). The Bible originated in God's thoughts and was communicated through his breath. It therefore has the same authority as God himself. We stand under the Bible's judgment rather than standing in judgment over it.

As God's authoritative Word, the Bible is complete, lacking nothing. No new revelation is needed or to be expected. It is the "faith which was once for all handed down to the saints" (Jude 3), our only infallible rule of faith and practice. In his Word we have been granted "everything pertaining to life and godliness" (2 Peter 1:3). Like the life-giving God, his Word is everlasting. As Jesus assured, "Heaven and earth will pass away, but My words will not pass away" (Matt. 24:35).

Since the life-giving God is "not a man, that He should lie" (Num. 23:19), his Word is true. The psalmist writes, "Your righteousness is an everlasting righteousness, and Your law is truth" (Ps. 119:142) and "The sum of Your word is truth, and every one of Your righteous ordinances is everlasting" (v. 160). Jesus prayed, "Sanctify them in the truth; Your word is truth" (John 17:17). Thus, as the church, we are to strive to be those who accurately handle "the word of truth" (2 Tim. 2:15).

In our postmodern culture, the question *Will it work?* often replaces the question *Is it right?* But churches that desire biblical church growth understand that while the first question is a practical necessity, the second always takes priority. What "works" may not always be "right." When faced with decisions and opportunities, life-giving churches make choices and take hold of opportunities on the basis of scriptural truth rather than the latest models, techniques, or methods, no matter how attractive.

The Bible is powerful and accomplishes the purposes for which God intended it (see Isa. 55:11). It bears witness of Christ (John 5:39) and equips for every good work (2 Tim. 3:16–17). Most important, it is the message that we preach. Paul writes, "When you received the word of God which you heard from us, you accepted it not as the word of men, but for what it really is, *the word of God,* which also performs its work in you who believe" (1 Thess. 2:13, italics mine). The Bible is what gives us the knowledge of God's will and his commission to go into all the world with the gospel.

Special revelation forms the foundation of our belief and is our only rule of faith and practice. On that foundation, common truths derived from the study of various fields of general revelation are added to develop the principles and core values from which eventual practices (methods and techniques) are developed. The level of practices, as illustrated below, is often the most visible and changing of the four levels. It is where seminars and workshops most often focus training. But practices are just the top, surface level. The essential nature of biblical church growth, which comes from the foundation of God's revelation, is missed if we use only the methods and techniques found at the practices level.

Development of Principles and Practices

General revelation helps explain why some churches that do not hold to the authority of Scripture are growing. By definition, churches that do not accept the Bible as authoritative cannot experience "biblical" church growth. Yet the question of growth goes deeper than such a simple pronouncement. In reality, common ground exists between believers and nonbelievers that comes from general revelation, in the sense that God "causes His sun to rise on the evil and the good, and sends rain on the righteous and the unrighteous" (Matt. 5:45). There are commonsense principles and practices that, when used properly, will produce results in any group. For example, many studies in the fields of business, human development, and sociology have concluded that people like to be welcomed and appreciated in a personal way. This principle is a common truth derived from general revelation that, when applied, works as well for a business enterprise as it does for a church.

Believe What You Know

After reading this far, you may be tempted to think that just believing in the authority of the Bible is enough to experience biblical church growth. Seeing the Bible as authoritative is crucial, but it must be noted that there are many churches that accept the Bible as authoritative that are not growing. The reason is that an acceptance of the Bible as authoritative is just one dimension of having the right premise. Another dimension must be added to see a complete picture of this principle of biblical church growth. That dimension is passion.

Studies conducted over the past three decades have shown that a church's passion in articulating its beliefs is a second dimension that affects a church's growth and/or decline. In the 1970s Dean Kelly completed a study called *Why Conservative Churches Are Growing*, in which he noted that churches that were passionate in their commitment to biblical teaching and behavior tended to grow more than those that were less passionate. Another study among Lutherans, published under the title *Courageous Churches: Refusing Decline, Inviting Growth*, reported that growing churches know what they believe (biblical authority) and believe what they know (passion). More recently, Thom

44

Rainer reported similar results in his book *Effective Evangelistic Churches* from a study among Southern Baptists. Addressing this issue, Kent R. Hunter writes, "It should be no surprise that the more liberal the articulation of Christian beliefs, the less the local church has grown. In other words, those congregations that are very clear in articulating their commitment to biblical teaching and Christian behavior actually are more attractive to unbelievers."[3]

In effect, a church that is committed to the authority of God's Word and is passionate in articulating its beliefs and behaviors has increased potential for biblical church growth. Such a church knows what it believes and believes what it knows. Its members and leaders have a clear biblical mandate for church growth from God's Word and a high desire to carry out their mission. The church may not actually experience growth because of not following other biblical principles of church growth, but it does have great potential for biblical church growth (see quadrant 1 in the figure below).

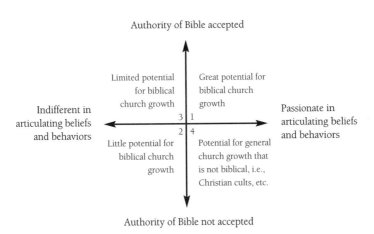

A church in the opposite quadrant (2) has little belief in the authority of God's Word and is indifferent in articulating its beliefs and behaviors. Such churches do not know what they believe and do not believe what they know, so few churches in this quadrant ever experience biblical church growth. The few that do grow do so primarily because of sociological or demographic changes outside of their control. A complete paradigm shift in the order of a spiritual revival would need

---

Smart Move

Using a large sheet of paper, make two columns with the headings in bold letters "Know What We Believe" and "Believe What We Know." Then under each heading list as many ways as you can think of that your church's ministry reflects each of the two aspects. How many church programs or ministries are in place to help people know what they believe? How many help people believe what they know? Under which column is your church the strongest? How can you begin to bring more balance between the two aspects of commitment to God's Word?

---

to take place in these churches for them to turn around with renewed vitality and growth. Unfortunately, this is the place in which many mainline churches find themselves today.

Churches that are more evangelical often face a different issue regarding belief in God's Word. Represented in quadrant 3, a number of these churches say they believe in the authority of God's Word. In practice, however, they do very little. Such churches know what they believe but do not always believe what they know. Just having a commitment to God's Word is not enough to experience biblical church growth. There must also be passionate involvement in following God's purpose and obeying his commands. Churches that find themselves in quadrant 3 often focus on the content of Scripture but show little emotion or reaction to such content. For example, a church may say that unbelieving people are lost and heading for an eternity without Christ but do almost nothing to share the life-giving message of Christ with them. Likewise they may believe in the power of prayer but commit little time to praying. Some of the churches in this quadrant may actually experience church growth if they happen to be in the right place at the right time using the right methods. But it is almost always by accident that they grow, since their lack of passion keeps them from doing anything by design that would help them experience biblical church growth.

The final quadrant (4) is where we find some cults of Christianity. As mentioned previously, some churches that hold a low view of biblical authority do grow. Part of the reason is related to their use of commonsense principles discovered from general revelation. Another reason has to do with their passion. Many cults are known for their strict beliefs, high demands, and passionate commitment. There is no doubt that their passion attracts unsuspecting believers as well as unbelievers who are searching for a sense of spirituality in their lives. The potential for growth among these churches is actually fairly high, but it is not biblical church growth. The growth of these churches can be compared to unhealthy physical growth in people, such as in obesity or cancer.

Biblical church growth is founded on the realization that the Word of God is "living and active and sharper than any two-edged sword, and piercing as far as the division of soul and spirit, of both joints and marrow, and able to judge the thoughts and intentions of the heart" (Heb. 4:12). The apostle Peter's words ring loudly: "For you have been born again not of seed which is perishable but imperishable, that is, through the *living and enduring word of God*" (1 Peter 1:23, italics mine). Churches that have a high commitment to the authority of God's Word and passionately communicate their beliefs to those outside the faith have great potential for biblical church growth, especially as they add other biblical principles to their church growth mix.

Touch our eyes that we may see the truth, and touch our hearts that we may burn with compassion, and steel our wills, good Lord, that we may do those things that we know we ought to do. This we ask in Christ's blessed name. Amen.

Donald A. McGavran[4]

Questions to Ask and Answer

1. How strong is your church's commitment to the Bible as God's authoritative Word?
2. In what practical ways is commitment to the authority of the Bible demonstrated in your church?
3. How passionate is your church in articulating its beliefs and behaviors?
4. In which of the four quadrants described in this chapter is your church found?
5. What ramifications does being in that particular quadrant have for the future growth of your church?
6. In which quadrant would you like to see your church?

FOUR

The Right Priority

Glorifying God

Bring speedily, O God, the time when every knee shall bow and every tongue shall confess that Your Son, our Saviour Jesus Christ is Lord to the glory of God the Father.

Donald A. McGavran

Early on the morning of July 4, 1952, thirty-four-year-old Florence Chadwick waded into the water off Catalina Island and began swimming toward California. Florence had already become the first woman to swim across the English Channel—both directions! Now she was attempting to become the first woman to swim the twenty-one miles across the San Pedro Channel.

The distance of the channel posed no difficulty for Florence, as she was physically well prepared for the challenge. A world-class swimmer, Florence was destined to be a member of the long-distance swimming hall of fame. Yet this day was to prove difficult.

Like many mornings in California, heavy fog blanketed the coastline as Florence stepped into the water off Catalina Island to begin her historic attempt. Several boats carrying her support team moved along with her as she swam into the channel. Some of her team went along to provide protection from the sharks, which needed to be driven away with rifle shots over the next few hours. Her mother and her trainer rode in one boat to provide encouragement to Florence when the swimming became difficult.

After swimming for nearly fifteen hours in the bone-chilling water, Florence asked to be helped into one of the boats. Physical fatigue was not a problem, but the icy waters had numbed her to the point of desperation. As she peered through her goggles to see the shoreline of California, all she could see was dense fog. On most days in Southern California, the fog lifts between 10:00 A.M. and noon. For some reason, this day was different, and the fog had not lifted by the time Florence neared the shore. Realizing that Florence was very close to achieving her goal, her mother and her trainer urged her to continue swimming. Fighting on for nearly another hour, Florence continued to look for the California coast, but all she could see was thick fog.

After swimming for fifteen hours and fifty-five minutes, she asked again to be hauled out of the water into a boat. Fearing for her safety, her team agreed to her request and helped her into one of the boats. When the boats arrived on the shore of the California coast, Florence was devastated to learn that she had been only one-half mile from her goal.

Later that day a reporter asked her why she had failed in her bid to swim the channel. She reportedly replied, "It was the fog. Look, I'm not excusing myself, but if I could have seen land, I know I could have made it."

Two months later, Florence was back on Catalina Island ready to make a second attempt at swimming the San Pedro Channel. Once again the fog covered the channel as she made her way into the water and began her struggle against the elements. Again the water was bitingly cold, and the fog never lifted. But this day was different. This day Florence succeeded in becoming the first woman to swim the San Pedro Channel. She even beat the men's record by two hours. Following her swim, she met with many newspaper reporters. During the questioning, one reporter asked what had been the difference between her first failed attempt and this second victorious one. She answered, "I made it this time because the shore was in my heart."[1]

> ## The Right Priority—Glorifying God
>
> Life-giving churches see their ultimate goal
> as bringing glory to the life-giving God.

The Ultimate Goal

Florence Chadwick's failure in her first attempt to swim the San Pedro Channel was not due to the cold water, the dangerous sharks that lurked nearby, or the twenty-one-mile distance. She failed because of the fog. The fog had obscured her view, her thoughts, and most of all, her heart. In short, she failed because she lost sight of her ultimate goal.

Preparing for a long-distance swim required the setting and accomplishment of numerous small goals. Florence had to obtain permission from the proper authorities to attempt the swim. She had to procure equipment, recruit volunteers, and coordinate schedules. A training timetable had to be arranged that would bring Florence to a peak point of readiness on the day of the attempted crossing of the channel. These and other short-term goals had to be met, but they all fundamentally aimed toward the accomplishment of one ultimate goal. On July 4, 1952, the ultimate goal for Florence Chadwick was to reach the shore of California. Even though she accomplished many of her smaller goals, she failed in the ultimate one. It was only when Florence was able to keep her ultimate goal clearly in mind and heart that she succeeded.

Achieving biblical church growth requires a similar discipline in keeping the right priority clearly in mind. There are a great number of goals that a church should seek to accomplish: winning the lost, building up the saints, preaching the Word, seeking justice, developing leaders, and many more. But there is only one ultimate goal: bringing glory to the life-giving God. Life-giving churches have the *right priority*—glorifying God. Simply stated, *life-giving churches see their ultimate goal as bringing glory to the life-giving God.*

51

It was formally stated in 1647 in the Westminster Confession and is now commonly accepted in the Christian church that "man's chief and highest end is to glorify God, and enjoy him forever."[2] Giving glory to God (Greek, *doxazo,* from *doxa*) means giving him credit for who he is, acknowledging his attributes and unchanging essence. The glory of God is all that God actually is (see Exod. 33:18–23), and our recognition of that actuality gives glory to him. We can give God glory in a multitude of ways, in our thoughts, work, songs, actions, prayers, lifestyles, and so on. Basically, whatever we do and say communicates our opinion of God to him and to others. All we do gives him either glory or dishonor. As Paul told the Corinthians, "Whether, then, you eat or drink or whatever you do, do all to the glory of God" (1 Cor. 10:31).

The necessity of giving glory to the life-giving God is a main theme throughout the Bible. "God Himself is a glorious being. Glory belongs to Him as light and heat belong to the sun."[3] God works in the lives of his people to bring glory to himself. As he says regarding Israel's affliction, "Behold, I have refined you, but not as silver; I have tested you in the furnace of affliction. For My own sake, for My own sake, I will act; for how can My name be profaned? And My glory I will not give to another" (Isa. 48:10–11). Therefore God's people are to give him glory. As David says when giving thanks, "Ascribe to the LORD, O families of the peoples, ascribe to the LORD glory and strength. Ascribe to the LORD the glory due His name" (1 Chron. 16:28–29). God's people are to give him glory throughout all time. As even the twenty-four elders attest at the end of the age, "Worthy are You, our Lord and our God, to receive glory and honor and power; for You created all things, and because of Your will they existed, and were created" (Rev. 4:11). The prime end of all things is the glory of God. It is only as we adopt this as our ultimate priority as individuals and corporately in our churches that we will live and function in complete harmony with the purposes of God.

Even the life-giving Savior's ultimate purpose in coming to earth was to bring glory to his Father. After entering Jerusalem riding on a donkey, the multitude met Jesus with cries of "Hosanna!" Shortly after, Jesus spoke to the people and said, "'Now My soul has become troubled; and what shall I say, "Father, save Me from this hour?" But for this purpose I came to this hour. Father, glorify Your name.' Then a voice came out of heaven: 'I have both glorified it, and will glorify it again'" (John 12:27–28). Later Jesus predicted that one of his disciples would betray him. After Judas had left the Lord's Supper, Jesus took the opportunity to explain, "Now is the Son of Man glorified, and God is glorified in Him" (13:31). Shortly thereafter, Jesus lifted his voice to heaven in prayer, and we listen in to the intimate conversation and discover how committed Jesus was to fulfilling his ultimate purpose of bringing glory to God. "Father," Jesus prayed, "the hour has come; glorify Your Son, that the Son may glorify You. . . . I glorified You on earth, having accomplished the work which You have given Me to do. Now, Father, glorify Me together with Yourself, with the glory which I had with You before the world was" (17:1, 4–5).

The church, of course, must fulfill the ultimate priority of its life-giving head. Writing to the church in Rome, Paul encourages the believers to bear the weaknesses of those without strength and not just to please themselves. Christ is to be our example. Even he did not please himself but sought to please his Father. Why is this important in the church? Paul explains his thoughts with these words: "Now may the God who gives perseverance and encouragement grant you to be of the same mind with one another according to Christ Jesus, so that with one accord you may with *one voice glorify the God and Father of our Lord Jesus Christ*" (Rom. 15:5–6, italics mine). As church members persevere together in loving care for one another, the church with "one voice" brings glory to God.

Showing kindness, such as providing financial support in times of need, also is a way the church brings God glory. Writing to the Corinthians concerning their gracious financial gift to the Macedonian believers, Paul tells them, "Because of the proof given by this ministry, they will glorify God for your obedience to your confession of the gospel of Christ" (2 Cor. 9:13).

In his second letter to the Thessalonians, Paul tells the believers how proud he is of them for their faith in the midst of persecution. Such trials are an indication of God's righteous judgment that will fall on unbelievers as well as believers. God allows the faithful to suffer persecution "so that the name of our Lord Jesus will be glorified in

---

Smart Move

If you have not done so recently, take the time this next week to do a short Bible study on the topic of God's glory. Later develop a teaching series on this topic and present it within the next twelve months to the entire congregation, an adult fellowship, or a small group.

---

you, and you in Him, according to the grace of our God and the Lord Jesus Christ" (2 Thess. 1:12).

Even the use of spiritual gifts has as its end the eventual glorification of God. The apostle Peter writes, "As each one has received a special gift, employ it in serving one another as good stewards of the manifold grace of God. . . . so that in all things God may be glorified through Jesus Christ, to whom belongs the glory and dominion forever and ever" (1 Peter 4:10–11).

Paul's letter to the Ephesians is the clearest expression of the ultimate priority of the church. Beginning in chapter one, Paul declares three times that the work of the Godhead in the church is directly related to God's glory. The Father's work of blessing, choosing, predestinating, and adopting is "to the praise of the glory of His grace" (Eph. 1:6). Our redemption through the Son's blood, whereby we receive forgiveness and inheritance, is "to the praise of His glory" (v. 12). We are sealed in Christ with the Holy Spirit as a pledge of our inheritance "to the praise of His glory" (v. 14). Paul then sums up the first half of his letter with these conclusive words: "Now to Him who is able to do far more abundantly beyond all that we ask or think, according to the power that works within us, to Him be the glory in the church and in Christ Jesus to all generations forever and ever" (3:20–21).

How the Church Glorifies God

How does a church bring glory to God? This can be done in numerous ways. We glorify God by worshiping him, "for we are the true circumcision, who worship in the Spirit of God and glory in Christ Jesus and put no confidence in the flesh" (Phil. 3:3). Indeed, "an hour is coming, and now is, when the true worshipers will worship the Father in spirit and truth; for such people the Father seeks to be His worshipers" (John 4:23). As members of the body of Christ, we are to present our bodies as "a living and holy sacrifice, acceptable to God" as a spiritual act of worship (Rom. 12:1).

Living a godly life also brings glory to God because we have been chosen to be "holy and blameless before Him" (Eph. 1:4; see also Col. 1:22). As living stones in the church, we are to "offer up spiritual sacrifices acceptable to God through Jesus Christ" (1 Peter 2:5). Using a similar thought, the writer of Hebrews says, "Through Him then, let us continually offer up a sacrifice of praise to God, that is, the fruit of lips that give thanks to His name" (Heb. 13:15). Being thankful brings glory to God. As the psalmist declares, "Whoso offereth praise glorifieth me" (Ps. 50:23 KJV).

Perhaps the most direct statement on how to glorify God was made by Jesus when he declared, "My Father is glorified by this, that you bear much fruit, and so prove to be My disciples" (John 15:8). Bearing fruit is important to God because "it is of the very essence and outflow of [Christ's] life."[4] "Wedded with this is the concept that God, the giver of all physical life, is also the source of all spiritual life and fruit."[5] God is a life-giving God, and our bearing fruit attests to his divine involvement in our life. In addition, bearing fruit brings a completeness to glorification that began with the Savior. God is glorified in two acts of work—the work of Christ and the work of the believers in bearing fruit. Leon Morris writes, "There is an air of completeness and of certainty about it. The disciples will surely glorify the Father by their continual fruit-bearing."[6]

According to Christ, bearing fruit is a primary way for his disciples to bring God glory. But what exactly is fruit? There are two dominant possibilities—character and converts. The first possibility is that Christ is referring to the fruit of the Spirit listed in Galatians. "But the fruit of the Spirit is love, joy, peace, patience, kindness, goodness, faithfulness, gentleness, self-control" (5:22–23). In support of this view is the fact that in his upper room discourse Christ uses some of the same words as are in the fruit of the Spirit list, such as peace (John 14:27), love (15:9), and joy (15:11). Each of these words, and the others found in the listing of the fruit of the Spirit, reflects attitudes that should be found in obedient Christians. This is a plausible explanation of what bearing fruit means and one that is held by a number of students of the Bible. However, while fruit clearly refers to Christian character traits in Galatians, from the larger context of John's Gospel, it does not appear to be what Christ had in mind.

A better explanation for the meaning of "fruit" in John 15 appears to be that it represents new converts or disciples. John's purpose in writing his Gospel is to show that Jesus Christ is the life-giving Savior who came to bring eternal life to all who would believe in him (see John 20:30–31). An illustration of Christ's concern for new converts is seen in his conversation with his disciples after conversing with the woman of Samaria (4:1–38). Just as the Samaritan woman was leaving to go back to her village, Jesus' disciples returned and "were amazed that He had been speaking with a woman" (v. 27). James Rosscup comments on their interaction: "He discerned that their primary interest was in satisfying their own personal, physical needs rather than satisfying the spiritual needs of others. He seized the golden opportunity to share with them His own sense of priority which elevated the Father's interests above all else" (see vv. 31–34).[7] "My food," Jesus said, "is to do the will of Him who sent Me and to accomplish His work" (v. 34). The Father's work, as we have already noted, was Christ's death on a cross as a provision for the salvation of all people.

As Jesus spoke with his disciples, he saw that the Samaritan woman was making her way back with a large crowd from the village. He used the opportunity to give a living demonstration to his disciples of what he wanted from them. Comparing the concept of harvesting souls to that of harvesting grain, Jesus pointed to the coming crowd and said, "Lift up your eyes and look on the fields, that they are white for harvest. Already he who reaps is receiving wages and is gathering fruit for life eternal" (vv. 35–36). The fruit Jesus was referring to was the new converts who came through the testimony of the Samaritan woman and Christ's own teaching. This is unmistakable from the following verses, which report: "From that city many of the Samaritans believed in Him because of the word of the woman who testified. . . .

And He stayed there two days. Many more believed because of His word" (vv. 39–41; see also Matt. 9:35–38).

Another indication that Christ was using the word *fruit* to mean new converts appears later in John 15. Jesus told his disciples, "You did not choose Me but I chose you, and appointed you that you would go and bear fruit, and that your fruit would remain, so that whatever you ask of the Father in My name He may give to you" (v. 16). While this statement is made in the midst of Christ's discourse on the disciples' need to love one another, it seems apparent that he was talking about winning new converts when he spoke of bearing fruit that should remain. That, of course, was the whole point of choosing and appointing the Twelve. Christ did not appoint the Twelve just to form a loving band of believers, although their love for each other was certainly important. No, Christ's appointment of the Twelve was to disciple the nations (see Matt. 28:16–20), which involved making new converts (fruit). In his well-known prayer found in John 17, Jesus mentions his commission of the twelve disciples when he prays, "As You sent Me into the world, I also have sent them into the world" (v. 18). Then, thinking ahead to the people who would be converted because of the disciples' obedience to his commission, he adds, "I do not ask on behalf of these alone, but for those also who believe in Me through their word" (v. 20).

John records the disciples' commission following the resurrection of Christ in 20:21, "Peace be with you; as the Father has sent Me, I also send you." Reading further in John 15, we see that the role of the Holy Spirit in empowering the witness of the Twelve is expounded: "When the Helper comes, whom I will send to you from the Father . . . He will testify about Me, and you will testify also" (vv. 26–27). Why did Christ select and appoint his disciples? Why did he send the Holy Spirit to empower them? The answer is to win new converts to Christ, converts who would remain his followers.

Within the Gospel of John it seems fairly clear that *fruit* means new converts. This interpretation of the word *fruit* has support in other New Testament books. For example, the apostle Paul wrote to the Romans, "I do not want you to be unaware, brethren, that often I have planned to come to you . . . so that I may obtain some fruit among you also, even as among the rest of the Gentiles" (1:13). At first glance, it may appear that Paul is talking about spiritual fruit, but a continued reading of the chapter points out that he is talking about converts. In verses 15 and 16 Paul explains: "So, for my part, I am eager to preach the gospel to you also who are in Rome. For I am not ashamed of the gospel, for it is the power of God for salvation to everyone who believes, to the Jew first and also to the Greek."

It is likely that Paul was thinking of new converts when he spoke of the "first fruits of Achaia" (1 Cor. 16:15). With his vast knowledge of Old Testament Scriptures, no doubt Paul used the language of Leviticus 23:10 intentionally. This passage instructs the people of Israel, "When you enter the land which I am going to give to you and reap its harvest, then you shall bring in the sheaf of the first fruits of your harvest to the priest." The people of Israel were to give the Lord the first part of the harvest, the first fruits, as a token of the full harvest yet to come. By saying the "first fruits of Achaia," Paul meant they were the first converts of that region, and more converts were to come!

Christ came to glorify God the Father by dying on the cross so that many people would be saved through his name. The image of the Lord as the living vine and the church (believers) as the branches is a perfect picture of the necessity of making countable disciples as an act of bringing glory to God.

One more point needs to be made, however. In Merrill C. Tenney's book on John, he writes: "Fruitfulness appears in obedience, which is a sure mark of the believer as disobedience is a mark of the unbeliever."[8] We are reminded in John 15 that fruit bearing comes from God alone: "For apart from Me you can do nothing" (v. 5), and "the branch cannot bear fruit of itself unless it abides in the vine" (v. 4). "He who abides in Me," Jesus declares, "and I in him, he bears much fruit" (v. 5). Bearing fruit requires that each of us abide in Christ. What it means to abide is explained in verse 10. "If you keep My commandments, you will abide in My love," Christ says. Thus *abide* alludes to being obedient and is repeated by the apostle John in another book in a similar context when he writes: "This is His commandment, that we believe in the name of His Son Jesus Christ, and love one another, just as He commanded us. The one who keeps His commandments abides in Him, and He in him" (1 John 3:23–24). Abiding is a lifelong journey of getting to know God and his Word and learning to walk in obedience to all his commands.[9] However, in the context of John 15, it seems likely that the main focus of abiding is directed toward obedience to the Lord's commission to be witnesses (Acts 1:8) and to make disciples (Matt. 28:16–20). The disciples who are obedient will "prove to be [Christ's] disciples" (John 15:8) by bearing much fruit.

The ultimate priority of the church is not its growth per se but the glory of God. Biblical church growth is similar to happiness. We never find happiness by searching for it. Happiness is discovered only as a by-product of some other endeavor. As we commit ourselves to our family, work, and a great purpose in life, happiness finds us.

The same is true of biblical church growth. Our priority must always be to bring glory to our life-giving God. As we invest our lives and energy in pursuit of this ultimate goal, and apply other principles of growth, biblical church growth will come to our churches as a by-product of our investment.

Bringing glory to God is not a nebulous idea that frees us to live a life of limited action. Rather, it involves specific expectations. It is expected that as members of Christ's body, we will obediently follow Christ by worshiping him, growing in our personal character, offering him praise, and living holy and blameless lives. Even more specifically, it means we will be obedient to Christ's command to make disciples, bearing fruit that will remain.

What is the best way to glorify God through fruit bearing? It is through having the *right process*, a principle that will be discussed in the next chapter.

Grant, we beseech You, to each of us Your special blessing as we study how to extend the church, how to multiply congregations, how to increase units of the redeemed, units of peace and justice in all peoples, all tribes, all castes, all classes of society, that praise and thanksgiving to Your glory may resound from every city and hamlet throughout the earth. In Christ's name we pray. Amen.

Donald A. McGavran[10]

Questions to Ask and Answer

1. Is the ultimate priority of your church to glorify God? If not, what is your church's ultimate priority? How do you know?
2. If bringing glory to God is your church's priority, can you list specific ways that this priority can be seen in your church's ministries or practices?
3. When you think of being faithful in bearing fruit, what do you mean—character or converts? Why?
4. How effective has your church been in seeing new people come to faith in Christ (bearing fruit as converts)?
5. If you were to rate your church's overall obedience to abiding in Christ on a scale of 1 to 10 (10 being the best rating), how would it rate? Why? What needs to be done to improve the rating?

FIVE

The Right Process
Discipleship

We seek church growth not for a bigger church or a better standing in the denomination, but for the purpose of seeing lost souls found and folded.

Donald A. McGavran

A few years ago, I was visiting a friend of mine in Portland, Oregon. We were sitting in his kitchen talking when the phone rang, and he answered it to begin what turned out to be a long conversation. To give him some privacy, I walked into the living room and sat down to read a magazine. About fifteen minutes later, a knock came on the front door. Since he was still talking on the phone, my friend stepped into the living room and motioned for me to answer the door. When I did, I found an energetic pastor who was canvassing the neighborhood door-to-door. As we began to talk, the pastor started to tell me about Jesus Christ and my need for salvation. Rather than let him go on, I interrupted to tell him that I already knew Jesus Christ as my personal Savior.

Delighted to find a fellow believer, the pastor began to tell me about himself and his ministry. He had come to Oregon from Virginia three years before to plant a new church. A core group of twenty-five believers had called him to be their pastor, and together they had successfully started a new church in the city of Portland. He shared how they had found a vacant church building to rent, about the various ministries they had started, and how faithful the church had been in winning new believers to Christ.

As he discussed the church's approach to evangelism, he noted that in the past twelve months 385 people had accepted Christ as their personal Savior through the church's outreach ministry. Since most churches report only one or two people coming to Christ in a twelve-month period, this report was indeed impressive. However, as we continued to talk, I casually asked how many people attended worship on an average Sunday morning. He replied, "Eighty-five people." My mind immediately raced back to the previous report that 385 people had come to Christ in the last twelve months. The contrast between the two figures startled me, and I inquired as to the reason for the disparity. In an embarrassed admission, the pastor agreed that while the church had seen many people come to Christ, not many had stayed in the church.

The church this pastor described evidenced a strong commitment to the Word of God. Not only did the members believe the Bible was God's Word, but they passionately shared their faith with others. In addition, they desired to do everything within their power to bring glory to God, particularly by bearing much fruit. It was clear. They had the *right premise* and the *right priority* to experience biblical church growth, but something else was not quite right. Jesus commanded his disciples to bear fruit that would remain (John 15:16). The church this pastor served was bearing fruit, but it was not remaining. This church was following the first two principles of biblical church growth but had neglected the third. They did not have the *right process*—discipleship! Simply stated, *life-giving churches make disciples by finding the lost, folding them into the body, and building them up in the faith.* They balance their disciple-making process around the three elements of evangelism, assimilation, and maturation.

62

> ## The Right Process—Discipleship
>
> Life-giving churches make disciples by finding the lost, folding them into the body, and building them up in the faith.

The Immediate Goal

Bringing glory to God is the church's ultimate goal. This is the highest work for his people. God is seeking those who will "be His worshipers" (John 4:23). Isaiah describes God's desire this way: "Bring My sons from afar and My daughters from the ends of the earth, everyone who is called by My name, and whom I have created for My glory, whom I have formed, even whom I have made" (43:6–7). To accomplish this mission of bringing worshipers to God, Christ gave his church an immediate goal—the Great Commission.

What has come to be called the Great Commission actually appears in the three Gospels of Matthew, Mark, and Luke. It is also mentioned in the Gospel of John and in Acts and is referenced in Romans. The most well-known and complete account is the one found in Matthew 28:16–20:

> But the eleven disciples proceeded to Galilee, to the mountain which Jesus had designated. When they saw Him, they worshiped Him; but some were doubtful. And Jesus came up and spoke to them, saying, "All authority has been given to Me in heaven and on earth. Go therefore and make disciples of all the nations, baptizing them in the name of the Father and the Son and the Holy Spirit, teaching them to observe all that I commanded you; and lo, I am with you always, even to the end of the age."

The context for the giving of Christ's commission is after his resurrection (vv. 1–15), just before he ascends into heaven. Apparently Jesus had told his disciples where to meet him (v. 16), and they obediently gathered at the designated place in Galilee. Galilee was a logical location for the meeting since it was the place of much of Christ's greatest ministry, such as the Sermon on the Mount and his transfiguration. When Jesus appeared, the disciples worshiped him, but some were doubtful (v. 17). Their doubt may have been an initial reaction to seeing Jesus, a doubt that was dispelled when he began to speak. It most likely indicates that more than just the eleven disciples were present, since the Eleven had already seen Christ (see John 20:29). More than five hundred of Christ's disciples may have been present for this final meeting (see 1 Cor. 15:6).

After the disciples were assembled, Jesus came forward and began to speak. Most statements of the Great Commission begin by quoting verses 19 and 20 of Matthew 28, but it is crucial to note that the context actually begins in verse 18, where Christ says, "All authority has been given to Me in heaven and on earth." As God, Christ always had ultimate authority, but when he came to earth as a baby, he "emptied Himself, taking the form of a bond-servant" (Phil. 2:7). Following his death, burial, and resurrection, Christ received special authority, as Paul adds in the Philippians passage:

> Being found in appearance as a man, he humbled himself by becoming obedient to the point of death, even death on a cross. Therefore also God highly exalted Him, and bestowed on Him the name which is above every name, that at the name of Jesus *every knee should bow,* of those who are in heaven, and on earth, and under the earth, and that every tongue should confess that Jesus Christ is Lord, to the glory of God the Father.
>
> verses 8–11, italics mine

In another passage Paul adds, "He raised Him from the dead and seated Him at His right hand in the heavenly places, far above all rule and authority and power and dominion, and every name that is named, not only in this age but also in the one to come" (Eph. 1:20–21). Christ's claim to all authority is unlimited, a fact stressed in the phrase "in heaven and on earth." Jesus has authority over all things in heaven, all things on earth, and everything in between. He alone has the active power to make authoritative statements and to reveal God's will. It is on his authority that the church will be built (Matt. 16:18).

After declaring that he has all authority, Jesus continues by saying, "Therefore . . . " (Matt. 28:19). The important point is that the disciples were no longer listening to a lowly itinerate preacher, but the King of Kings. They were no longer in the presence of a condemned

64

man hanging on a wooden cross, but the resurrected Savior. They were no longer following the humble carpenter from Nazareth, but the Lord of Lords. Therefore, what is the Ultimate Authority going to say? Is he going to say, "Love your neighbor as yourself" or "Feed the hungry," or perhaps "Seek justice for the oppressed"? All of these are important, but Christ says none of these. He says, "Go therefore and make disciples of all nations, baptizing them in the name of the Father and the Son and the Holy Spirit, teaching them to observe all that I commanded you" (vv. 19–20).

In order to understand this passage, it is necessary to have a basic understanding of the grammatical structure of the sentences.[1] Christ's command is in the form of an imperative in the main verb "make disciples," which is surrounded by three participles (go, baptize, teach), which are used to describe what must be done to fulfill the command.

A disciple is a learner or a pupil. Christ's call to discipleship is recorded as early as Matthew 11:29, when he said, "Take My yoke upon you and learn from Me." To be a learner is to be a disciple. Thus Christ's command was for the disciples to enroll others in his school, assisting others in becoming learners (disciples) of Christ. This word for making disciples is an exceptional word that is used only four times in the New Testament and only in the Great Commission as a command. The word *disciple* implies not only acquiring knowledge but living out what one learns. To be a disciple is to be a committed adherent who is personally involved in carrying out the will of the master.

The command to make disciples is accompanied by three other verbs in the form of participles. The first participle, "going," describes action that is concurrent with the imperative verb "make disciples." It picks up the force of the command and is thus correctly translated as an imperative "go." Without the action of "going," it is impossible to make disciples. It makes the command definite and intentional. It is not, "If you happen to be going," but "Go!" This indicates a sense of urgency. Followers of Christ are to take the initiative in making disciples of all the nations. We are not to wait casually for some accidental contact, but we are to go. It is logical to assume that "going" must take place before a disciple can be made; thus it presupposes the idea of winning others to Christ or evangelizing. It also implies that believers are to spend time with unbelievers, building life-giving relationships with them.

Baptizing and teaching logically follow the imperative to "make disciples," and these two parallel participles describe the means by which disciples are made. Each time a person is won to Christ through going, he or she is to be baptized and taught. The two words are in the present tense, which indicates that baptizing of all new converts is to be a continual event, and teaching them is to be an ongoing process. Baptizing implies a bonding of new believers to Christ and his church, while teaching implies the continual maturation of all believers as they are taught all things. Thus Christ commands us to assist people to become disciples (learners) by taking the initiative in sharing the gospel with the unsaved (go!) and then helping them bond with his body (baptize) and helping them mature in their faith (teach).

The scope of the command is to be carried out in "all nations" (*panta ta ethne*). *Ethne* is translated "nations" but should not be understood as a political nation, such as the United States of America or Argentina or Zambia. Our English word *ethnic* comes from the Greek word *ethnos* (singular of *ethne*) and refers more precisely to a tribe, people, family, or ethnic group.[2] Christ's commission echoes the promise to Abraham that through him, "all the families of the earth will be blessed" (Gen. 12:3). It predicts the song of the twenty-four elders recorded in Revelation 5:9: "Worthy are You to take the book and to break its seals; for You were slain, and purchased for God with Your blood men from every tribe and tongue and people and nation." The idea of a nation (*ethne*) is very flexible but most likely refers to a cohesive unit of people as large as a tribe or as small as a family clan. The idea is that as God's people, we are to be making disciples in every definable family, clan, or people group in the world. Reading Psalm 96 with this understanding of nation in mind brings forth a new understanding of God's ultimate purpose in bringing glory to himself.

> Sing to the LORD a new song;
> Sing to the LORD, all the earth.
> Sing to the LORD, bless His name;
> Proclaim good tidings of His salvation from day to day.

Tell of His glory among the nations,
His wonderful deeds among all the peoples.

· ·

Ascribe to the LORD, O families of the peoples,
Ascribe to the LORD glory and strength.

Psalm 96:1–3, 7

The Great Commission ends with a promise from the One who has all authority. "And lo, I am with you always, even to the end of the age" (Matt. 28:20). This promise is significant for a number of reasons. First, it tells us that the Great Commission is for us today. Over the centuries, some have taught that the Great Commission was only for the eleven disciples and that when they died, the Great Commission was voided. By promising his presence to the end of the age, Christ saw those who were listening to him as representatives of all who were to follow him in the future. Since the eleven apostles died before the fulfillment of the Great Commission, Christ's promise, as well as his command, cannot be limited to them alone.

> Remember that at the heart of the Church Growth Movement here or anywhere in the world is the Great Commission. We must never lose sight of this perspective which encompasses the whole world, every human being.
>
> Donald A. McGavran[3]

Second, the promise tells us that Christ is continuing to use his power to build his church (16:18). He will continue to empower his followers until his church is built to his satisfaction.

Third, it tells us that his followers will never be alone, no matter where they are. Literally, the passage reads, "I myself am with you always." By adding the emphatic "myself," Jesus lets us know we will never be alone. He guarantees our success in making disciples, since, as the one who has all authority, he will be with us to the end. The Great Commission is founded on the fact that Jesus Christ has been given all authority. On this power we base our hope, and this power is with us until the end of the age.

The Meaning of Discipleship

Biblical church growth views discipleship as the process of finding and winning the lost, folding them into a local church, and building them up in the faith. This process comes directly from Christ's command to "make disciples." The Holy Spirit indicates a clear process in the three participles that accompany the imperative command. The chart below shows the relationship of these verbs to the command.

Make Disciples

	Go	Baptize	Teach
Matthew 28:19–20:	Go	Baptize	Teach
Theologically:	Salvation	Identification	Sanctification
Programmatically:	Evangelism	Assimilation	Education
Personally:	Believing	Bonding	Maturing
Popularly:	Finding	Keeping	Building

As the chart shows, the three verbs *go, baptize,* and *teach,* have varied, though similar, implications, depending on how they are used. *Go* implies the action of winning unbelievers to Jesus Christ. Other words that convey a similar idea are *salvation, evangelism, believing,* and *finding. Baptize* refers to the action of becoming part of the community of faith. There is a twofold identification for the new believer; he or she is to identify with Christ (Rom. 6:3–11) and to identify with a local church (Acts 2:41). Other words that relate to this action are *identification, assimilation, bonding,* and *keeping. Teach* refers to the process of spiritual development. Other words that describe this process are *sanctification, education, maturation,* and *building.*

Essential to a full understanding of the Great Commission is an awareness that all of these actions rightfully fall under the umbrella called discipleship. Inherent in discipleship is the idea of a process that moves from believing to bonding to maturing. Theologically and strategically, the order of process moves from going to baptizing to teaching. Of course, in actual ministry situations, the process may not always follow the same pattern. However, biblical church growth is most often found in churches that develop a process of discipleship that takes into consideration all three of these actions rather than simply focusing on only one of them.

Smart Move

Take a sheet of paper and make three columns labeled "Finding," "Keeping," and "Building." Then think about each ministry or program your church conducts in a twelve-month period. For each ministry or program you identify, determine which column it fits under and list it there. When you have finished, carefully look over your lists. What do the lists tell you about your church's ministry? Where does your church place most of its emphasis? Which of the three areas is the weakest? Which is the strongest?

Finding Lost People

Biblical church growth is based on the belief that God wants his church to grow, and that growth should come primarily through evangelizing the lost. The imperative "go" logically comes before the command to "make disciples." If we don't go, we won't find lost souls and be able to make disciples. The Father's priority is apparent in the life of Jesus Christ, who came to seek and save the lost (Luke 19:10). The birth, life, death, burial, resurrection, ascension, intercession, and ultimate return of Jesus Christ are all tied to the desire of the Father to find the lost and bring them into reconciliation with himself. Arthur Glasser comments on this:

> The crucifixion and resurrection of our Lord are inherent to the record of the gospel of Jesus Christ. And yet, the events surrounding his cross and empty tomb do not climax the gospel narratives. The climax is his issuance of the mandate to disciple the nations. And this mandate is to be obeyed. Jesus Christ expects us to give ourselves to the task of gathering the lost.[4]

If we are to gather the lost, we must give evangelism first priority in the process of making disciples. We must proclaim Jesus Christ as God and Savior and persuade people to become his disciples and responsible members of his church.

Last century this principle led to a debate as to whether the higher priority should be given to evangelism or to social action. Today's emerging generation of missionaries, church planters, and church leaders does not see a distinction between evangelism and social action. They believe the two endeavors must be intertwined as we bring the Good News to the lost. To the younger generation, evangelism is not lost in a plea for social concern, and social concern is not separated from the eternal destiny of the lost. In their minds Jesus Christ came to bring salvation to the lost, but he also healed, fed, and cared for the unfortunate along the way. Christians must be concerned about bringing care, justice, and healing to people and to our world—meeting the needs of the poor and lost and managing our environmental resources in redeemable ways. However, while evangelism and social action are closely wedded, making disciples implies a logical priority of finding the lost. Before people can develop a heart for love and justice, they must experience the renewing work of salvation through belief in Jesus Christ.

Keeping New Believers

Once people are won to Christ, the next step involves bonding them to a local church so they can develop their identity as disciples. A new believer bonds first of all to Jesus Christ. This is the believer's primary identification. As Paul writes, "Do you not know that all of us who have been baptized into Christ Jesus have been baptized into His death? Therefore we have been buried with Him through baptism into death, so that as Christ was raised from the dead through the glory of the Father, so we too might walk in newness of life" (Rom. 6:3–4). This baptism takes place in the life of every true believer in Jesus Christ. Our new identity in Christ becomes the basis for our new way of life, as Paul points out in the rest of the paragraph: "For if we have become united with Him in the likeness of His death, certainly we shall also be in the likeness of His resurrection, knowing this, that our old self was crucified with Him, in order that our body of sin might be done away with, so that we would no longer be slaves to sin, for he who has died is freed from sin" (Rom. 6: 5–7; see also Col. 2:8–15).

There is a secondary identification, however, that takes place through baptism—uniting with the body of Christ. Following Peter's sermon on the day of Pentecost, we read, "So then, those who had received his word were baptized; and that day there were added about three thousand souls" (Acts 2:41). We must ask, *to what were the early believers added?* The context clearly shows they were added to the church in Jerusalem. The Christian life is not a solo affair. It is meant to be a life lived in community.

In a sense, salvation has both an individual and a corporate dimension. The life-giving God existed from eternity in community (Gen. 1:26–27). He created man and woman to live in community with each other and with himself (2:15–25). But sin destroyed the fellowship of their community relationship (chap. 3) and continued to disrupt future attempts at rebuilding a loving community after the fall (see the story of Cain and Abel in chap. 4). Thus part of Christ's call is to develop a new community of faith—the church—a community where the new commandment reigns.

Christ put it this way: "A new commandment I give to you, that you love one another, even as I have loved you, that you also love one another. By this all men will know that you are My disciples, if you have love for one another" (John 13:34–35). Biblical church growth realizes that this Great Commandment is to be obeyed and that the power to build community comes from those who have been regenerated. Thus the initial priority must be given to the Great Commission. In fact one of the motivations for taking the gospel to all nations is to bring people into biblical community with God and with other believers. For example, the apostle John writes:

> What was from the beginning, what we have heard, what we have seen with our eyes, what we have looked at and touched with our hands, concerning the Word of life—and the life was manifested, and we have seen and testify and proclaim to you the eternal life, which was with the Father and was manifested to us—what we have seen and heard we proclaim to you also, *so that you too may have fellowship with us; and indeed our fellowship is with the Father, and with His Son Jesus Christ.*
>
> 1 John 1:1–3, italics mine

Humankind was created to be in relationship. There is no biblical warrant for an independent believer living in isolation from other believers. The church is a community of believers called out of the world and into relationship with each other. Biblical church growth is a process that unites new believers with other believers in a local community—the church.

The power of authentic community empowered the witness of the Jerusalem church and resulted in even more church growth. Luke reports: "They were continually devoting themselves to the apostles' teaching and to fellowship, to the breaking of bread and to prayer. . . . And the Lord was adding to their number day by day those who were being saved" (Acts 2:42, 47). Underlying all the foregoing is the biblical church growth conviction that "God wants His lost children found and enfolded" into local churches.[5]

Maturing the Saints

The elements of discipleship include evangelization (go), assimilation (baptize), and education (teach). At its root, the word *disciple* means "learner," and learning is to be a continual process—a lifelong process of learning all that Jesus taught (Matt. 28:20). Jesus set the example, for as he traveled about, he was teaching, and great multitudes followed him (see 4:23–25). The early church devoted themselves to "the apostles' teaching" (Acts 2:42). The apostle Paul strengthened the souls of the disciples (14:22) in part by teaching "publicly and from house to house" (20:20).

Teaching includes a wide range of activities and subject matter. Much of the Christian life is learned from life circumstances (Phil. 4:11), by the teaching of the Holy Spirit through the Scriptures (John 14:26), and through human tutors (Phil. 4:9). Believers teach one another as they meet together in community (Heb. 10:25), using their spiritual gifts (see 1 Corinthians 12; Romans 12). Through teaching, the church reproduces faith and develops leaders for the future (1 Tim. 4:11–16; 2 Tim. 2:2). Biblical church growth occurs where believers are matured through the active teaching and preaching of the life-giving Word of God.

Discipleship is a process that involves all three of these elements—going, baptizing, and teaching. If a church focuses on only one of the three, it will have difficulty seeing biblical church growth take place. Some churches do a fine job of winning people to Christ; however, because they do little in the way of assimilation, they end up with few people to teach. Other churches focus on the teaching of believers but find few new converts coming into their fellowship to be taught. Still others stress a warm welcome but find people leaving after awhile due to the shallow teaching. Churches that experience solid biblical church growth will have a process that gives balanced emphasis to all three of these areas.

The Disciples' Response

The Great Commission is given in the Gospel of Mark in this way: "Go into all the world and preach the gospel to all creation" (16:15). The word "go" in this passage is also a participle, but the central command is "preach the gospel." It is also given in the Gospel of Luke in this manner: "Thus it is written, that the Christ would suffer and rise again from the dead the third day, and that repentance for forgiveness of sins would be proclaimed in His name to all the nations, beginning from Jerusalem. You are witnesses of these things" (24:46–48). This passage combines the two ideas of preaching (noted in Mark) and taking the gospel to all the nations (noted in Matthew).

John does not mention the Great Commission directly in his Gospel but appears to make reference to it when he quotes Christ saying, "I chose you, and appointed you that you would go and bear fruit" (15:16; see also 15:27; 20:21; 17:18). The geographical dimension is supplied in Acts 1:8: "But you will receive power when the Holy Spirit has come upon you; and you shall be My witnesses both in Jerusalem, and in all Judea and Samaria, and even to the remotest part of the earth."

The Great Commission is also referenced by Paul as he concludes his letter to the Romans. Note the inclusion of the elements of the Great Commission when he writes: "Now to Him who is able to establish you according to my gospel and the preaching of Jesus Christ, . . .

according to the commandment of the eternal God, has been made known to all the nations, leading to obedience of faith" (Rom. 16:25–26). Combined, these different statements of the Great Commission point out that Christ commands us to go and preach the gospel to those who do not know Jesus Christ as Savior, make disciples by assimilating into local churches those who believe, and then help them grow to maturity by teaching them all the things he commanded.

After hearing the Great Commission, what did the early disciples understand Christ to be telling them? How did they respond to his Great Commission? Their response is in the story of the Book of Acts. Sometimes called the Acts of the Apostles, it is also the Acts of the Holy Spirit as he empowered the believers to fulfill Christ's Great Commission. Following the empowering work of the Holy Spirit, three thousand people heard the preaching of the gospel, believed, and were baptized (Acts 2:41–42). As the church came together in authentic community, more people believed and were added to the church daily (v. 47). Their continued preaching of the gospel caused many of those who listened to believe, and "the number of the men came to be about five thousand" (4:4). When the church faced a difficult ethical problem and handled it with careful discipline, "more believers in the Lord, multitudes of men and women, were constantly added to their number" (5:14). As the church grew, a management crisis arose in the use of church resources that had an undertone of ethnic strife. The disciples managed the situation with wisdom, and "the word of God kept on spreading; and the number of the disciples continued to increase greatly in Jerusalem, and a great many of the priests were becoming obedient to the faith" (6:7).

The persecution of the church led to the gospel spreading to the Samaritans (8:5), the Ethiopians (vv. 25–40), and the Gentiles (11:20–26). The gospel spread through families, villages, and towns (16:14–40); all the while the "word of the Lord continued to grow and to be multiplied" (12:24; see also 19:20). The disciples took the gospel to all the nations (panta ta ethne). The gospel spread to Lydda, Sharon, and Joppa (9:35, 42). The message went to Samaria (8:5, 12) and into Phoenicia, Cyprus, and Antioch (11:19–26). The growth of the church expanded into all families, clans, tribes, and tongues because God does not wish "for any to perish but for all to come to repentance" (2 Peter 3:9).

The disciples were careful to teach all that Christ commanded them. The Book of Acts records not only the numerical and geographical growth of the church but also its spiritual growth. The inner life of the first church is carefully detailed in Acts 2:42–47. The believers' boldness in prayer (4:23–31) and the way they faced persecution (5:27–32; 7:59; 16:19–25) bear witness to their developing inner life. The actions of the disciples who had received Christ's Great Commission give evidence that they expected to see the church grow numerically, geographically, and spiritually.

Healthy Churches

Biblical church growth is concerned with the planting, multiplying, nurturing, and renewing of healthy churches. However, while no one desires to be part of a church that is unhealthy, we must ask the question, *Can a church be healthy if it doesn't grow?* In some situations it may be possible, especially in locations where the church is highly persecuted. Yet even in countries where the church is not free to assemble publicly, an underground church often experiences numerical growth. In the great majority of church situations, it would be difficult to think a church could honestly be labeled "healthy" if it was not growing by making countable disciples. Not only did Jesus Christ categorically state that he would build his church (Matt. 16:18), thereby sovereignly guaranteeing church growth, but he left us with a command to "make disciples," thereby sovereignly giving us a part in church growth. The desire to have a healthy church is normal, but numerical growth must be seen as one indication of such health. *Church growth* is the point! Healthy churches demonstrate both numerical and spiritual growth. Leaders who desire to see biblical church growth in their church must be careful not to allow an inward focus on renewing the health of their church to become an excuse for a lack of numerical growth.

An overemphasis on renewing the spiritual health of a church can actually make that church sick. When a church focuses on spiritual

---

The Bottom Line

Renewal, in and of itself, is no guarantee of growth. Renewal is a good thing. One could scarcely have too much. We all need to live in greater contact with the Savior, to know more of the Scripture, and to be more yielded. However, unless our renewal results in winning the lost, in giving first priority to time to share Christ, it is ingrown and falls short of what Christ requires.

McGavran and Arn[6]

---

renewal for too long, it becomes self-centered and loses a sense of mission. This happens because it develops a centripetal (inward) momentum that seeks to turn ever more inward. A centripetal church may maintain a vibrant life for a time, but without an outward focus, it will eventually collapse in on itself in selfish introspection. In contrast, churches that pursue biblical church growth develop a centrifugal (outward) force that focuses on making disciples. The challenge of winning new people to Christ forces church members to pray for open doors for the gospel and to seek answers to real-life questions that nonbelievers ask. An outward focus drives members into a closer and deeper relationship to Christ. It might be argued that a church could focus outwardly too much, which also would not be healthy. While this is a distinct possibility, it is seen infrequently. A historical analysis of churches shows that the greatest danger is too much of an inward focus. The biggest challenge for church leaders is not how to get people to study the Bible more but how to get people to evangelize more. It is not how to get people to focus on their own needs but how to get them to focus outward on the needs of others.

Biblical church growth is a journey, not a destination. A destination indicates the conclusion of a journey. If we reach our destination, the journey is over. This can never be the case with church growth, since God's purpose to seek and save the lost never ends here on earth. As long as there are lost people who need to be found and brought to Jesus Christ, the need for church growth will always be valid. Our churches must never stop growing. The only perfect church is the one still on the journey—a journey of obedience to the Great Commission.

Almighty God, You look out on all the people of earth, the unbelievable, incomprehensible multitudes of men and women with an equal eye. You regard them all as equally your lost sons and daughters who must hear the words of life and through belief in Jesus Christ your Son our Savior be brought back to their Father's House, the church of Jesus Christ. Grant to us a similar passion. Give us a reckless determination to reach the unreached with the Gospel of redemption. Then, Lord, give us knowledge and courage, and a great endurance. In Christ's Name we pray. Amen.

Donald A. McGavran[7]

Questions to Ask and Answer

1. How important is the Great Commission in your personal life and in the life of your church?
2. Describe ways your church is seeking to be obedient to Christ's commission. Are any of these ways bearing fruit?
3. Does your church have a process for finding, keeping, and building people that is working? Why or why not?
4. Would you say your church is a centrifugal church or a centripetal church? Why?
5. Is your church healthy? How do you know? What criteria do you use to determine whether it is healthy or sick?

SIX

The Right Power

The Holy Spirit

The growth of the Church is always brought about by the action of the Holy Spirit.

Donald A. McGavran

In his book *The Life God Blesses,* Gordon MacDonald shares a parable about a foolish man who built a sailboat. In a desire to own the most impressive boat among the members of his boat club, he spared no expense in outfitting his new craft. As MacDonald describes it, the man "outfitted his craft with colorful sails, complex rigging, and comfortable appointments and conveniences in its cabin. The decks were made from beautiful teakwood; all the fittings were custom-made of polished brass."[1]

After months of hard work, the day arrived for the launching and first voyage of the magnificent sailboat. Going with tradition, the boat was christened with a bottle of champagne broken against its bow. Members of the boat club cheered wildly from dockside. When the boat weighed anchor and the wind gradually filled the colorful sails, the boat sliced quickly through the calm waters of the harbor into the oncoming waves of the ocean.

For a time the man sailed smoothly along, enjoying the cool breezes coming across the bow of his new craft. As he basked in the glory of his accomplishment, the time slipped by, and he did not notice the increasing strength of the waves and force of the wind. His inexperience on the open ocean resulted in his being caught in a sudden storm. Gallantly he tried to return to port, but it was too late. Just a few minutes after he made his turn for home, a large wave hit the boat, and it capsized. A voyage that had started with so much fanfare and confidence ended in catastrophe.

Most sailboats right themselves after capsizing, but this man's did not. What was the problem? The boat eventually washed ashore, and the resulting investigation revealed that the boat had a fatal flaw—more weight above the waterline than below. In his effort to build the most impressive craft in his boat club, the man had invested all his resources on the topside of the boat so others could see its extravagant beauty. He chose not to invest below the waterline because he thought it unnecessary. Without proper ballast under the sailboat, however, it could not right itself after it capsized. Although this story is simply a parable, it illustrates that the way a boat, a person's life, or a church looks on the surface does not always tell the entire story.

Most of us have known people and churches that looked healthy on the surface but did not have enough spiritual weight "below the waterline" to remain stable. One church I am familiar with became a popular model by attracting an average attendance of over three thousand on Sundays. It appeared that all was well until a series of disruptions created undue pressure on the ministry and its leaders. Within a matter of four weeks, more than one thousand people fled the church, and within three months another thousand departed. While the church still averaged 1,200 worshipers each Sunday, the church body went into shock due to the loss of so many people. Over the next two years, the leaders sought to discover what had gone wrong. Their investigation revealed that while the church sponsored a number of programs that attracted visitors, they had forgotten to build "below the waterline." As the church grew, the leaders became reliant on the effective programming and neglected to build up the spiritual strength of the worshipers. A vibrant emphasis on prayer was lost in the haste to begin additional programs. Classes and small groups where people could gather to pray were neglected. Since the leadership had focused mainly above the waterline, when the church capsized, it had too little spiritual weight to right itself.

Failure to build below the waterline is not just a problem of larger churches. Small churches can also fall into this trap. One discouraged pastor revealed to me how he had gone to a fifty-five-member church determined to put prayer at the forefront of the ministry. Each day when he arrived at his office, he would spend the first thirty minutes in prayer for the church. He made sure that prayer became a vital part of all areas of the church's life, and he put many new programs into place. Over a five-year time span, however, he and the church slowly forgot to pray. By the end of the fifth year, he was coming to the office and getting right to work, neglecting his prayer time. Church meetings opened with perfunctory prayer so that the members could get on to the real business at hand. The church had begun to focus solely on the strength of its programs and personnel. Two years later the pastor left for a new ministry in a different state, and the church leaders dropped every program he had started. While some of the pastor's programs had produced numerical growth, the deeper levels of spiritual motivation had been neglected. The programs themselves were not sufficient stimulus to keep the people ministering, so when they experienced burnout, the programs were discontinued.

Not all stories are negative. I was invited to speak at one of the fastest growing churches in Southern California. The assimilation seminar began at 7:00 P.M. and ended at 10:00 P.M. on a Friday evening. The people were receptive to what I had to say, yet it was what took place after the meeting that caught my attention.

When the meeting ended, I stepped down from the platform and began talking with the senior pastor about the church. While we spoke, I noticed that several individuals began removing the tables and chairs from the conference room. When the room was finally cleared, the doors were opened and hundreds (yes, hundreds) of people started coming into the room. Most had a Bible that they placed in front of them on the floor as they knelt down and began to pray. After watching for a few minutes, I turned to the senior pastor and asked, "What's going on?"

He replied, "All-night prayer meeting."

The Right Power—the Holy Spirit

Life-giving churches trust in the sovereign work
of the Holy Spirit for the growth of the church.

"All-night prayer meeting?" I asked. "Tell me more."

Sensing my interest, the pastor explained how the church met every Friday evening for an all-night prayer meeting. A few hundred church leaders assembled each Friday to seek God's face and to ask for his blessing on the church ministry. Ministry leaders also met for prayer in the early morning each day of the week. From the senior pastor's viewpoint, the reason the church had grown so dramatically was due to the prayer of the people. While the pastor, staff, and members of this church worked hard in the ministry, through their emphasis on prayer, they demonstrated trust in Christ as the builder of his church. The leaders understood a crucial fact of biblical church growth—God is the one who builds his church.

The Life-Giving Spirit

What cannot be observed in a church is often more important than what can be. That is why churches that desire to experience biblical church growth rely on the *right power:* the Holy Spirit. Put simply, *life-giving churches trust in the sovereign work of the Holy Spirit for the growth of the church.*

Along with the Father and the Son, the Holy Spirit was integrally involved in bringing life to the world. The life-giving work of the Holy Spirit began at creation. At the beginning of creation, "the earth was formless and void, and darkness was over the surface of the deep, and the Spirit of God was moving over the surface of the waters" (Gen. 1:2). The psalmist teaches that the Holy Spirit continues to exercise active care over creation: "You send forth Your Spirit, they are created; and You renew the face of the ground" (Ps. 104:30).

The Holy Spirit was the empowering agent that brought into being the life-giving inspired Word (2 Tim. 3:16). Many of the writers of the Bible tell how the Holy Spirit directed their speaking and writing. For example, David wrote, "The Spirit of the LORD spoke by me, and His word was on my tongue" (2 Sam. 23:2). Using a similar image, God tells Isaiah, "My Spirit which is upon you, and My words which I have put in your mouth shall not depart from your mouth, nor from the mouth of your offspring, nor from the mouth of your offspring's offspring" (Isa. 59:21). In his first sermon on the Day of Pentecost, the apostle Peter noted that the Holy Spirit inspired David: "Brethren, the Scripture had to be fulfilled, which the Holy Spirit foretold by the mouth of David concerning Judas, who became a guide to those who arrested Jesus" (Acts 1:16). Later Peter explained how the Holy Spirit empowered all the writers of the Bible: "But know this first of all, that no prophecy of Scripture is a matter of one's own interpretation, for no prophecy was ever made by an act of human will, but men moved by the Holy Spirit spoke from God" (2 Peter 1:20–21).

Jesus was empowered by the Holy Spirit from the beginning of his earthly life. As Isaiah prophesied, "Then a shoot will spring from the stem of Jesse, and a branch from his roots will bear fruit. The Spirit of the LORD will rest on Him" (Isa. 11:1–2; see also 42:1–4; 61:1–2). Mary was with child "by the Holy Spirit" (Matt. 1:18), the "Spirit of God" descended on Jesus at his baptism (3:16), and he was directed into the wilderness by the Spirit to be tempted by Satan (4:1). Even Jesus' preaching and miracles were accomplished in the Holy Spirit's power (Luke 4:14–21; Matt. 12:18, 28; Acts 10:38).

The Holy Spirit is called the "Spirit of life" (Rom. 8:2) and is the power Christ uses to bring salvation to those who believe in him. "He saved us, not on the basis of deeds which we have done in righteousness, but according to His mercy, by the washing of regeneration and renewing by the Holy Spirit" (Titus 3:5). Indeed, "unless one is born of water and the Spirit he cannot enter into the kingdom of God" (John 3:5).

The Holy Spirit is the "Spirit of truth" (14:17) the Father sent to believers after Christ ascended to heaven. The Holy Spirit's primary role is to bring glory to Christ, and he does this in part by bringing to our remembrance what Jesus taught (16:12–15). The Spirit seals (Eph.

1:13), indwells (Rom. 8:9–11), and fills (Eph. 5:18) the believer for effective life and ministry.

The Holy Spirit inaugurated the church (Acts 1:5 and 2:4) and empowers its witness. As Christ promised, "You will receive power when the Holy Spirit has come upon you; and you shall be My witnesses both in Jerusalem, and in all Judea and Samaria, and even to the remotest part of the earth" (1:8). It is the convicting work of the Holy Spirit that leads people to Christ (see John 16:8–11). In truth, no biblical church growth has ever been experienced without the presence and power of the Holy Spirit.

Not by Human Effort

Churches that follow biblical church growth principles know that God sovereignly promised the growth of his church (Matt. 16:18) and that such growth comes through the life-giving work of the Holy Spirit. It is not because of human effort, as God revealed through the prophet Zechariah by saying, "Not by might nor by power, but by My Spirit" (Zech. 4:6).

God's Word through Zechariah to Zerubbabel was in reference to the rebuilding of the temple following the Babylon captivity. According to tradition, Zerubbabel had been given permission to rebuild the temple after he won a contest in which the main object was to prove what was the strongest thing in the world. Having argued successfully that truth was the strongest thing in the world, Zerubbabel likely put great confidence in his own reasoning abilities.

Zerubbabel apparently had a history of starting projects and never finishing them. Whenever his projects encountered difficulties, he would get discouraged. Predictably, he faced unseen problems in rebuilding the temple. The challenges appeared as overwhelming as mountains, and he once again became discouraged. It was at this point that God intervened with a message of encouragement through the prophet Zechariah.

"Not by might," God begins. The word *might* (*hayil*) has the basic meaning of "strength" and is often translated "power" or "ability." At other times it is translated "army," "host," "company," "train," or "retinue," which may suggest that might is derived through organizational strength. When used in this context, it "seems to have the force of the methods or techniques—the strategies by which might is put into effect."[2] "Nor by power," God continues. The word *power (koah)* overlaps a great deal with *might*. Contextually, the word refers to personal prowess or potency. It means personal force and "includes the idea of an individual's strength of body, character, and personality."[3]

God told Zerubbabel not to trust in the might of his methods, techniques, and strategies or in the power of his own personality—emotional, mental, or spiritual. Note that God does not say these things are bad. Indeed, they are necessary. It would have been folly for Zerubbabel to attempt to rebuild the temple without a strategy. Visionary projects require that proper techniques and methods be employed.

> Churches which
> grow are
> Churches which
> seek earnestly
> the gracious
> power of God.
>
> Donald A. McGavran[4]

God also did not say Zerubbabel was to rid himself of personality. Indeed, that would have been impossible. Significant projects require that real people invest emotional, mental, and spiritual energy to accomplish them. The point? Zerubbabel was not to *depend* on these things.

"But by My Spirit," God concludes. The little word *but* indicates a major contrast between Zerubbabel's might and power and God's Spirit. Zerubbabel's work was to be accomplished by a totally different means—by the Holy Spirit. Zerubbabel's techniques, methods, and strategies were not useless—if totally controlled by God's Spirit. His personality was not useless—if totally abandoned to God's Spirit. God promised Zerubbabel if he would move forward with total trust in the Holy Spirit, then the difficulties that looked like mountains would become for him "a plain; and he will bring forth the top stone with shouts of 'Grace, grace to it!'" (4:7).

Churches that wish to experience biblical church growth will use proper techniques, methods, and strategies. Their leaders will use the power of their personalities in setting vision and direction for the future. But such churches and leaders will carry out their responsibilities in total dependence on the work of the Holy Spirit. As we have seen, Jesus said, "*I will build* My church." Paul confirmed the

---

F.Y.I.

Churches have been holding prayer meetings for years, but in many cases they haven't seen growth, because Christians seldom petition God for growth. They don't pray specifically for the conversion of close friends and loved ones. They don't pray for families by name. They don't pray that new churches will be planted. They don't pray for the discipling of young believers. In other words, they don't pray intelligently for growth.

Donald McGavran and Win Arn[5]

---

primacy of God's role in church growth when he stated, "I planted, Apollos watered, but *God was causing the growth*" (1 Cor. 3:6, italics mine). The growth of Christ's church is "something that takes place in the world through the agency of the Holy Spirit working through countless dedicated servants of God and a diversity of institutions and organizations."[6]

Building below the Waterline

It is the life-giving work of the Holy Spirit that empowers church programs, plans, and strategies. Churches that rely solely on human personality and ingenuity may grow for a time, but their growth will have little spiritual weight beneath the surface. This is because some churches rely too heavily on human analysis and projections. Some may become enamored with human methodologies and blueprints. Leaders may even become prideful with bloated egos. This is not what God intends. Churches that seek biblical church growth remember that apart from Christ they can do nothing, not even build a church (see John 15:5). To build a church that glorifies God requires that he be at the center of the process. Methods and personalities will take a church only so far. If God is not intimately involved below the waterline, the church will eventually capsize.

The enthusiastic acceptance of pragmatic methods, strategies, and models during the past has left the impression among observers that church growth adherents cared more about strategy than the Spirit's working. While in some cases this may have been true, church growth leaders have always affirmed that there is no biblical church growth apart from the work of the Holy Spirit. Donald McGavran asserts, "The growth of the Church is always brought about by the action of the Holy Spirit. As in the New Testament Church, so today, the Holy Spirit leads, convicts of sin, converts, builds up, selects missionaries and thrusts them out to ripened fields. The concern of Christians today must be to understand the workings of the Holy Spirit and to be open to His leading."[7]

> Church growth will always contain an element of mystery that defies all human penetration, analysis, and definition and that casts us back on the Head of the church in prayer, trustful waiting, and patient labors.
>
> George W. Peters[9]

Recent studies have confirmed again that prayer is a vital factor in the growth of churches, and a new interest has developed in stressing the spiritual factors of church growth.[8] Fresh ideas have surfaced regarding traditional prayer elements, such as fasting, prayer chains, prayer partners, prayer concerts, prayer summits, prayer retreats, prayer in small groups, and prayer meetings. New developments in spiritual warfare, such as strategic-level warfare, prayer evangelism, spiritual mapping, prayer walking, mobilization of intercessors, concerts of prayer, on-site praying, and two-way prayer have been accepted by many churches, although these developments remain controversial to some. While churches will adopt different positions on prayer and spiritual warfare issues, the key fact is that when churches tap into the power of the Holy Spirit, they have great potential for biblical church growth. About technique, Carl George says, "Church growth is more a matter of heart first and then of having a certain technique."[10]

How do churches that desire biblical church growth tap into the Holy Spirit's infinite supply of strength? Through prayer! "Neglect prayer and we neglect the health and vitality of our churches."[11] Prayer

Smart Move

Organize prayer teams for each of the pastoral staff and other key leaders, such as Sunday school workers and children's ministry personnel. Triads seem to work best, with two prayer partners for each leader. Have the prayer teams pray for each other on a daily basis and meet monthly for an hour of personal sharing and prayer. This teamwork provides a prayer covering for leaders and strengthens their reliance on the Holy Spirit's empowerment for faithful ministry.

is an attitude as well as an activity, and churches seeking biblical church growth "pray without ceasing" (1 Thess. 5:17). Luke carefully records the fact that a prayerful attitude and activity permeated the life of the Jerusalem church. After Christ gave the Great Commission, one hundred and twenty of the disciples returned to Jerusalem, where they "were continually devoting themselves to prayer" (Acts 1:14), and prayer continued to be a major aspect of their worship (2:42). The apostles prayed publicly at the temple (3:1) and practiced prayer as a vital part of their leadership duties (6:4). Leaders were chosen and appointed through times of prayer (6:6; 13:2–3), and crises were faced with prayer (12:5).

Today churches that desire biblical church growth place prayer at the forefront of their ministry. Prayer is the key to discerning and correcting some of the barriers that block a church's growth. It is the discipline that helps us grow nearer to God's heart. Yet it is vital to point out that "prayer is not so much an effort as a communion."[12] It is seeking the face of God. It is listening to what he has to say to us, more than our asking him to bless our plans and goals. God told Solomon that his people should "humble themselves and pray and seek My face and turn from their wicked ways, then I will hear from heaven, will forgive their sin and will heal their land" (2 Chron. 7:14).

God was speaking to Solomon particularly about Israel, but the principle is applicable to today's church. Biblical church growth is found in churches that seek God's face; that is, they listen to his direction. Seeking God's face requires that churches set aside their agendas. It means not trusting in their own wisdom and power to strategize and "make things happen." It means communing with God through prayer until their will becomes his will. When leaders commit their work to the Lord, they are acknowledging that "the mind of man plans his way, but the LORD directs his steps" (Prov. 16:9).

Perhaps this is one of the reasons some churches have not found church growth principles fruitful. They have been trying to make them work in their own wisdom and power. The problem is not with biblical church growth principles but with the attitude or motive of the churches and/or their leaders. There is a difference, of course, between human power and spiritual power, and leaders throughout history have struggled with the challenge of appreciating the difference. Jacob manipulated the blessing from his father, Isaac, and stole it from his brother, Esau (Genesis 27). Jacob's practice of making things happen permeated his life until he wrestled with God in a place Jacob later named Peniel—"face of God" (32:24–30). Jacob had to learn to trust God rather than himself, and he learned this when he saw God's face. As he said, "I have seen God face to face" (v. 30). Jacob's newfound humility is seen in his restored relationship with his brother, Esau, in the following chapter (33).

Seeking God's face is a metaphor describing our submission to God's will and leading in our lives and churches. Both Moses and Peter had to learn such submission to God's will. Moses tried to take matters into his own hands to free the Israelites living in Egypt and ended up committing murder (Exod. 2:11–14). After Moses had spent forty years in the desert herding sheep, God met him at the burning bush and commissioned him to lead his people out of Egypt (Exodus 3). It was through this experience with God that Moses was empowered, and then in God's power, not his own, Moses returned to Egypt and accomplished the mission.

In his own strength the apostle Peter told Jesus, "Even though all may fall away because of You, I will never fall away" (Matt. 26:33). Later, on the night Jesus was betrayed, Peter sought to prove his might by taking matters into his own hands, and "having a sword, drew it and struck the high priest's slave, and cut off his right ear" (John 18:10). Yet his personal wisdom and power failed him that same night when someone recognized him as one of Jesus' followers and he responded by denying Jesus three times (Matt. 26:69–75). Following the resurrection, in a conversation with Jesus, Peter revealed a different attitude, and Jesus restored him to ministry (John 21:15–17).

One of the reasons more churches do not experience biblical church growth is tied to this truth: *They have not sought the face of God.* They are seeking growth through their own wisdom and power rather than by submitting themselves and their church to the Holy Spirit's direction.

Seeking God's face in prayer—asking for his guidance—implies a search for God's will rather than our own. In some churches the prayer focus is almost entirely on temporal issues. Physical health problems and church struggles fill up the agendas for prayer. In churches that seek biblical church growth, these temporal issues are not forgotten but are balanced with concern for the salvation of the lost. Prayer in growing churches focuses on issues of eternity, and patient intercession keeps a finely tuned focus on the lost. In these churches time is spent seeking God's help and direction in the best ways to win the lost rather than asking God to bless what the people have decided to do on their own.

> One of the reasons more churches do not experience biblical church growth is tied to this truth: *They have not sought the face of God.*

This reflects Paul's example. He desired and prayed for the salvation of his brethren (Rom. 10:1). He instructed Timothy that prayers should be offered for all because God "desires all men to be saved and to come to the knowledge of the truth" (1 Tim. 2:4). Paul asked the Colossians to pray that God would "open up to us a door for the word, so that we may speak forth the mystery of Christ" and to pray that "I may make it clear in the way I ought to speak" (Col. 4:3–4). He tells the Ephesians to "pray on my behalf, that utterance may be given to me in the opening of my mouth, to make known with boldness the mystery of the gospel" and "that in proclaiming it I may speak boldly, as I ought to speak" (Eph. 6:19–20). All of these passages mention prayer in the context of reaching the lost. We are, of course, to pray for spiritual growth, but we seem to do that more naturally. Prayer for effective evangelism requires regu-

---

Another Smart Move

Have people in your church make individual lists of all their friends who do not know Jesus Christ as their Lord and Savior, but who live close enough to attend your church. Once the lists are written, encourage your people to pray weekly for each of the persons named on their list, praying specifically for one year for each person's salvation. Four times during the year, offer a nonthreatening outreach event—for example, a concert, seminar on parenting, or sports dinner—to which your people may invite those on their prayer lists to come and hear the gospel.

---

lar emphasis, because if evangelism is not first in our hearts, it usually does not even make the list.

Effective Prayer

There is no simple formula for effective prayer, but there are biblical examples of people who prayed effectively. One person who stands out in this respect is Daniel. As one who always sought the face of God, his prayer in Daniel 9 offers three basic principles that every church should strive to implement.

First, *churches seeking biblical church growth are to pray in the light of God's Word.* Daniel's prayer was based on his study of Jeremiah's writings that the captivity of God's people was to last only seventy years (Dan. 9:2). Daniel prayed to God concerning the direct implications of God's Word on his contemporary situation. If our prayers are based on our own selfish desires, our confidence in prayer will be weak. If, on the other hand, our prayers are consistent with the revealed will of God in the Bible, our confidence will be strong.

Second, *churches seeking biblical church growth are to pray in humility.* Daniel writes that he gave "attention to the Lord God to seek Him by prayer and supplications, with fasting, sackcloth and ashes" (v. 3). This shows that Daniel sought the face of God with humility. Prayer

90

was serious business for Daniel. His prayers were not just addendums to a meal or meeting but humble praise and petition offered in the awareness of God's awesome presence. When we can pray believing that the God of the universe is listening, we can pray with confidence.

Third, *churches seeking biblical church growth are to pray in light of God's character.* Daniel begins with confession and then grounds each of his petitions in the character of God. He asks for the return of Israel from Babylon, based on the faithfulness and immutability of God's promises (vv. 7, 15). He asks God to take away his wrath from Jerusalem on the basis of God's righteousness (vv. 7, 14, 16). He intercedes for the land, relying on the compassion of the Lord (vv. 9, 18).[13] When we trust in God's unchanging character, we can pray with confidence.

Churches with different traditions and perspectives regarding prayer and the Holy Spirit will no doubt approach this biblical church growth principle somewhat differently. However, to be effective, their prayers must be true to God's Word, offered with a measure of humility and seriousness, and based on the character and nature of God. As Daniel prayed using these principles of effective prayer, God began to answer his requests (vv. 19–23). No doubt, he will answer our prayers for biblical church growth when they are offered in like manner.

When prayer is the foundation of a church's words, decisions, and actions, that church gives God glory for whatever growth occurs. As churches faithfully build below the waterline through effective prayer, the life-giving nature of the Holy Spirit empowers biblical church growth.

Almighty and everlasting God, You have called a people for Yourself from the ends of the earth. Grant the increase of Your rule and Your passion among us and pour out Your Holy Spirit upon us that Your name may be proclaimed to all who sit in darkness and the shadow of death.

Donald A. McGavran[14]

Questions to Ask and Answer

1. Whom are you trusting to bring about the growth of your church? How do you know?
2. Is your church building above the waterline or below it?
3. In what specific ways do the leaders of your church model dependence on God for church growth?
4. How strong is the personal prayer life of your congregational members, church leaders, and pastoral staff? Cite some examples.
5. Would you say the corporate prayer life of your church is vibrant or dull? Why?

SEVEN

The Right Pastor
A Faithful Shepherd

The minister in our churches must not do evangelism by himself. His duty is rather to train other Christians to do it.

Donald A. McGavran

"I want you to know that my church is a healthy flock," advised the pastor of an older, three-hundred-member church. "We're not winning people to Christ, but we're healthy. There's too much emphasis on numerical growth nowadays anyway. I think we need to focus on helping people grow spiritually. If we're healthy enough spiritually, numerical growth will come naturally."

A discouraged pastor of a small neighborhood church complained, "There is no way we can grow in this location. There are two megachurches in our community, and there is no way we can compete with their programs. Besides, people in our community aren't interested in church anymore. If we were in a different location, we could probably grow, but not here."

"I don't want this church to grow any more," declared the pastor of a new church plant. "I've already got too many people with too many problems, and I can't handle any more. I believe God wants us to focus on being faithful with the flock we already have rather than seek to increase our membership."

These comments represent statements I have heard numerous times. Each one expresses a common theme of pastors who believe that God may want other churches to experience church growth, but they somehow rationalize that growth cannot happen in their churches. It should come as no surprise that the pastors who made the previous comments did indeed see no growth in their churches. In part, the lack of growth in the churches these pastors serve is a self-fulfilling prophecy. As a wise person reportedly said, "If you believe you can or believe you can't, you're right!"

Research on churches over the last quarter century has consistently revealed that one of the central differences between growing churches and declining churches is a pastor who believes God wants his church to grow.[1] Put another way, a crucial variable for biblical church growth is the leadership of the local pastor or the senior pastor of a multiple-staff church.

Working with God

The importance of growth leadership first became apparent to me some years ago when I began attending a church three blocks from my home. The pastor was a good Bible teacher with expertise in biblical prophecy. However, he did little to lead the church toward growth, lacking what some people call vision. Church members appreciated his knowledge of the Bible but were concerned over the church's lack of direction. During his tenure, the church actually declined in membership to a point where the future of the church looked bleak. Some members were even talking of closing the church due to the low attendance. Eventually, through a series of circumstances that could only be described as God's leading, the pastor left the church.

After a year of struggling along, the church called a new pastor, who also excelled as a Bible teacher. During his first year of ministry, he began to move the church toward a renewed commitment to the Great Commission. Gradually the board members and people in the church teamed together to initiate new outreach events in the community.

Within three years, the church relocated to a major street in the city that provided better visibility and accessibility. By the end of the pastor's fourth year of ministry, the church was averaging a very healthy 350 in worship. For nearly two decades he faithfully led the church toward biblical church growth. While the church he served never became well known, the pastor remains to this day a significant model of a faithful shepherd.

It is amazing the difference a leader's attitude can make in the life of a church. The change in the health and vitality of this particular church revolved around the leadership attitudes of the two pastors. Both were godly men who loved and taught the Bible with excellence. However, one believed in taking the initiative to work with God to see his church grow, while the other sat back to see what God would do.

There is an old story about two farmers who were talking together alongside a field that was yielding a bountiful harvest. The farmer who owned the land was predictably proud of the crop. As farmers are prone to do, he talked incessantly to his friend about the trials and tribulations that went into the plowing, fertilizing, planting, irrigating, and harvesting. When the farmer finally stopped talking, his friend commented, "Yes, God has certainly done a good job on that field." The other farmer replied, "True, but you should have seen it before God hired me."

Few farmers I am aware of would claim to be able to grow a crop all on their own. Most would give God the credit. However, we all realize that the harvest would not be very profitable if the farmer just sat back to let God do the work alone. Can you imagine a farmer who purchased seed but then let it sit in the barn all year? Can you imagine a farmer who did no plowing, fertilizing, irrigating, weeding, or harvesting? What kind of harvest would result from such a lack of effort? It would be a very poor one indeed. God is the one who grows the crop, but he does so in cooperation with the farmer. It is when a farmer faithfully plows, fertilizes, plants, and irrigates that God produces a harvest.

In similar fashion, God has chosen to work with earthly leaders to accomplish his purpose of bringing life to a lost world and glory to his name. The apostle Paul in his letter to the Corinthians specifically

95

notes this fact. Jealousy and strife had risen among the Corinthians. They argued among themselves and began to choose sides, some saying they followed Paul and others, Apollos. After chiding the Corinthians for their immaturity (1 Cor. 3:1–4), Paul told them, "I planted, Apollos watered, but God was causing the growth" (v. 6). Taking sides was inappropriate, because God was the ultimate cause of growth and deserved all the glory. Paul and Apollos did, of course, have a part in cooperating with God in bringing life to a lost world. God could have selected other means of communicating the life-giving message of salvation to lost people, yet he determined to work through earthly leaders to grow his church. They were God's "fellow workers" (v. 9).

God-Given Leadership

Leadership has always been a major factor in the growth of God's kingdom. This is seen in the books of the Bible that carry the names of God's leaders, such as Joshua, Ruth, Nehemiah, Matthew, James, and John. Other biblical books also tell the stories of God's leaders, as in Acts, which begins with Peter, introduces Philip, moves to Stephen, and continues on to Paul. Even a casual reading of the Bible reveals that God works through leaders to accomplish his mission. That is why the fifth principle for biblical church growth is the *right pastor:* a faithful shepherd. Simply stated, *life-giving churches are led by pastors who faithfully serve as God's fellow workers in fulfilling the Great Commission.*

The metaphor of the flock is widely used in the Bible, sometimes of Israel (Jer. 13:17), once of the disciples (Luke 12:32), and several times of the church (Acts 20:28; 1 Peter 5:3). Jesus Christ is the shepherd of his flock and knows each of his sheep (John 10:27). God gave Christ "as head over all things to the church" (Eph. 1:22), and he is therefore its Chief Shepherd and primary leader (1 Peter 5:4; see 2:25 and John 10:11). Christ has absolute and final authority over the whole church and every detail of its plans. As the Chief Shepherd, he is to be consulted regarding decisions that must be made. His will is to be sought as new plans and methodologies are selected. He is to be a constant presence and steady guide to each local assembly.

The Right Pastor—A Faithful Shepherd

Life-giving churches are led by pastors who faithfully serve as God's fellow workers in fulfilling the Great Commission.

One outgrowth of Christ's authority is his appointment of leaders, or under-shepherds, for the local churches. Although people all over the world make up Christ's universal flock, he sees them as local flocks shepherded by local pastors. These shepherds are responsible for their local church, a fact that Peter acknowledges when he tells elders to "shepherd the flock of God *among you*" (1 Peter 5:2, italics mine).

Referring to these earthly shepherds, Paul writes that Christ "gave some as apostles, and some as prophets, and some as evangelists, and some as pastors and teachers" (Eph. 4:11). These terms are not describing spiritual gifts but rather gifted individuals whom Christ gives to his church as leaders. As pastors serve local churches under Christ's headship and by his appointment, they are to represent his interests and lead according to his agenda rather than their own.

Christ gives leaders to the church "for the equipping of the saints for the work of service, to the building up of the body of Christ" (v. 12). As the Chief Shepherd, he has committed the tending of his flock to under-shepherds (John 21:15–17; 1 Peter 5:2; Acts 20:28). They are to live, dream, breathe, and labor for the building up of the church. They do this by equipping the individual believers in local congregations for ministry and mission in the world. As the church is shaped through the work of the Holy Spirit in the people, the church grows. The underlying idea is that the church will not grow—numerically or spiritually—without the catalytic involvement of leaders. Noted missiologist Charles Van Engen explains:

> Leadership as an event involves the movement of a local group of God's people toward participating in God's mission in the world. As such, it includes the leader as a catalyst to stimulate the followership of the people in a mutually agreed direction in the midst of a particular spiritual, social, economic, political, and cultural context. In the midst of it all, the Holy Spirit, as the One who constitutes and mobilizes the Church, uses

the entire mix of complex factors to move God's people to be and do something new in the world. God-given leaders are in the center of all that happens when the event of leadership occurs.[2]

The pastor of a local church has a high calling and an awesome responsibility. The sheep will follow his lead, and he dare not lead them astray. He must study and teach the Word of God in order to feed the flock. He must know the mind of Christ in order to utter, "Thus saith the Lord." He must lead the church to fulfill Christ's mission of seeking and saving the lost. No local church will experience growth if the under-shepherd is not in agreement with the mission of Christ. Similarly no church will grow if the sheep do not follow the under-shepherd's lead.

Dynamic Elements of Leadership

One of the most helpful examples of a shepherd is King David. The psalmist's commentary on God's calling David to be the king of Israel is instructive: "He also chose David His servant and took him from the sheepfolds; from the care of the ewes with suckling lambs He brought him to shepherd Jacob His people, and Israel His inheritance. So he shepherded them according to the integrity of his heart, and guided them with his skillful hands" (Ps. 78:70–72).

Note first of all that David is God's servant. Leadership exerted by God's under-shepherds is servant leadership. God had seen David give faithful service in shepherding the ewes and lambs of his earthly father and knew he would shepherd Israel with the same heart. Building on a similar theme, Peter tells earthly pastors to "shepherd the flock of God among you, exercising oversight not under compulsion, but voluntarily, according to the will of God; and not for sordid gain, but with eagerness; nor yet as lording it over those allotted to your charge, but proving to be examples to the flock" (1 Peter 5:2–3). This passage reveals that a servant's heart will have at least three attitudes. First, *servant-leaders serve due to God's calling—not under compulsion*. Second, *servant-leaders serve to bring God profit—not for sordid gain*. Third, *servant-leaders serve with humil-*

The Bottom Line

Leadership is an essential consideration in church planting and growth. When we have the right people in the right positions—people who are qualified in character and who have a biblical philosophy of ministry—churches will grow not only numerically but also spiritually.

Gene Getz and Joe Wall[3]

---

ity—*not lording it over the flock*. David was such a pastoral servant-leader.

As a pastoral servant-leader, David led Israel with integrity. The word *integrity (tom)* is often translated "soundness," "simplicity," and "uprightness." It seems to carry the meaning of sincerity of heart and motive. Therefore it is roughly equivalent to *character*. The central idea is that David had an inner goodness and purity of life that led to a life of correct thinking, feeling, and behaving. David's character played a major role in God's selecting him to be king and in his leadership ability over Israel.

David also led Israel with skill. The word *skillful (tebunah)* refers specifically to one's discerning and reasoning ability. It is derived from a root word *(bin)* that carries the idea that discernment can be learned through training and observation. David was skillful with his hands, which indicates he was competent in the practical, how-to skills necessary to carry out leadership functions. Not only was David a person who could be trusted, but he had the ability to manage Israel's resources, oversee its leaders, command its army, and represent its foreign affairs.

Biblical church growth requires pastors who will shepherd the flock of God with character (integrity of heart) and competence (skillful hands). Character is mentioned first because it is the overriding crucial dimension for biblical leadership. No wonder Paul instructs Timothy: "An overseer, then, must be above reproach" (1 Tim. 3:2). Shepherds are to be selected on the basis of their character. "This component of the pastoral servant-leader speaks about *who we are*, not professionally, not intellectually, not in task, not in strategy—but *person-ally*."[4] Competence is also necessary for a church to be led effectively. The moral and ethical failure of a pastor will devastate a church, but a godly pastor who is incompetent is no blessing.

It Takes Teamwork

Three words are used synonymously in the Bible for Christ's under-shepherds or leaders: *overseer, elder,* and *pastor*. These three terms indicate nuances of the same responsibility. An overseer *(episkopos)* is one who literally stands above and looks out over all that is before him. It implies an ability to give care by creating the organization and governance to accomplish a given vision. Elder *(presbyteros)* refers to one who is experienced or aged. It points to a quality of wisdom gained from having lived long enough to experience a significant number of life events. Pastor *(poimen)* is a shepherd, essentially one who leads and cares for a flock of sheep. The implication is that God's under-shepherds are to watch over and guide a particular group of God's people. The duty of the under-shepherd is to feed, protect, and lead the flock (see Acts 20:28).

From the beginning of his church-planting ministry (Acts 14:23) until the end (Titus 1:5), Paul expected each local church to be led by a team of under-shepherds. He told Titus to "appoint elders in every city," and a plurality of elders is observed in Ephesus (Acts 20:17; 1 Tim. 3:1–7; 5:17–25), in the church at Philippi (Phil. 1:1), and in the churches located in Crete, Pontus, Galatia, Cappadocia, Asia, and Bithynia (Titus 1:5; 1 Peter 1:1; 5:1–2). The Bible seems to support a multiple team of pastors, whether they are paid or volunteer.

While the need for a strong initiating leader who serves a church with integrity of heart and skillful hands is well documented in church growth studies,[5] biblical leadership almost always takes place within a team structure. Research by church growth leader Win Arn has shown that effective under-shepherds are good communicators, goal-oriented, self-motivated, able to build a team, open to change, willing to take logical risks, and certain of a call to ministry. They have a solid family and clear priorities, and they relate well to people. Each of those ten aspects of a faithful under-shepherd is important, but being able to build a team may be one of the most crucial. A careful study of strong leaders in the Old Testament reveals that one of the reasons for their success was that they worked well with teams. Moses led the children of Israel with a team composed of Aaron, Hur, Joshua, and the seventy elders (Exod. 4:14–16; 17:8–13; 18:13–23). King David operated with a team of godly people (2 Sam. 23:8–39), and Ittai, Zadok, Abiathar, Hushai, and Ziba supported him during his exile (15:19–16:4). Nehemiah assembled a team of Ezra (Neh. 8:1–9), Hanani, Hananiah, Shelemiah, Zadok, Pedaiah, and Hanan (1:2; 7:1–2; 10:23; 13:13).

In the New Testament, teamwork is evident in Jesus' ministry with the twelve disciples (Matt. 10:1) and in Paul's ministry with coworkers Barnabas, John Mark, Timothy, Luke, Titus, Erastus, Priscilla, Aquila, Silas, and others (Acts 15:40; 19:22; Rom. 16:1–23; Col. 4:7–14; 2 Tim. 4:10–13). Teams form the context of effective leadership through all ages.

The existence of a team of leaders does not eliminate the role of a special leader. In fact the best teams have great leaders. Within the framework of a team of elders, or whatever term your church uses to describe your leaders, there is a great diversity of gifts. Some elders will be administrators, others will be excellent teachers, and some will focus on exhortation, giving, or some other area of service to the body of Christ. A few will be highly visible, while others will remain in the background. And, yes, some will be leaders of the team. "There is a tacit assumption on the part of the congregation that these leaders will have more visibility and more to say about the organization than the average person."[6]

Note the twelve disciples as an example. All of the Twelve were equal in terms of their office and privileges, yet there was diversity in their roles in ministry. These differences show up in the various lists of the Twelve (Matt. 10:2–4; Mark 3:16–19; Luke 6:14–16; Acts 1:13). Each list divides the Twelve into three groups of four names. The three sublists always contain the same names, although the order is somewhat different. In each list the first name in each subgroup is always the same. In the first group Peter is listed first, in the second group Philip, and in the third James. Apparently each of the subgroups had a recognized leader. His position as leader was not necessarily by appointment but resulted from his unique influence on the group. The Twelve were equal in calling, office, and honor. They all healed, preached the coming kingdom, and had access to Jesus, but some stood out over the others as leaders among leaders. This does not imply their spiritual superiority, but it does imply superior influence.

A strong team needs a leader to update the vision and communicate it to the larger congregation. The leader of the team is the entrepreneur, deciding when to move forward with new projects and when to hold back. The leader is the coach, challenging the team to think bigger and to raise the bar of excellence. The leader is the architect, reviewing plans and arbitrating between divergent goals and directions. It is proper for the elders to have a strong, influential leader, who may be the senior pastor. Peter obviously provided this for the disciples, as did Paul and Barnabas at other times for their own teams. Moses was uniquely gifted as the leader of his team, as were Nehemiah and others.

Pathfinding

The vitality of a local church is in large measure related to its being on the path that the Chief Shepherd has revealed. In fact a common phenomenon in declining churches is an atmosphere of aimless drifting.[7] Thus a primary role of an under-shepherd is to lead a church in discerning an appropriate path of ministry. The central responsibility of leadership is pathfinding. The key focus of pathfinding is not influence, personality, or persuasion, nor is it analysis and planning. The key focus is mission, that is, determining what the mission of the church is and then designing ways to fulfill the mission. Big ideas need a champion, and leaders must be the champions of the church's mission. In this role they cast a vision of a preferable path to the desired goal. A pastor is leading when he is pointing to some future possibility, communicating that possibility to others, and himself moving toward what might be. Only when someone points beyond what is now to what can be does leadership take place.

Leading a church toward fulfillment of Christ's mission requires faithful stewardship. Paul writes, "Let a man regard us in this manner, as servants of Christ and stewards of the mysteries of God. In this case, moreover, it is required of stewards that one be found trustworthy" (1 Cor. 4:1–2). People are fond of saying, "We are not called to be successful but faithful." They are right! Faithfulness to God and his mission is most important.

The Greek word for steward (*oikonomos*) is a combination of the words "to manage" (*nemo*) and "house" (*oikos*). It literally means "to manage a house." A good example of a steward who manages a house is found in Genesis. Joseph was the steward of Potiphar, who "made him overseer over his house, and all that he owned he put in his charge" (Gen. 39:4). Later when he became Pharaoh's chief administrator, Joseph had his own steward (44:1–4). A steward often had full charge of his master's affairs, including educating the master's children and handling his business affairs (see Matt. 20:8).

Pastoral servant-leaders are responsible for stewarding (or faithfully managing) the mysteries of God. The phrase *mysteries of God* refers to something that was hidden in former times but has now been revealed and initiated by Christ.[8] The writings of Paul indicate that the "mystery" is the gospel. The main responsibility of God's undershepherds is to be stewards of the message of Christ's death, burial, resurrection, and soon return. This is the message that Christ commanded should be taken to all the nations, as Paul expresses:

Now to Him who is able to establish you according to my gospel and the preaching of Jesus Christ, according to the revelation of the mystery which has been kept secret for long ages past, but now is manifested, and by the Scriptures of the prophets, according to the commandment of the eternal God, has been made known to all the nations, leading to obedience of faith; to the only wise God, through Jesus Christ, be the glory forever. Amen.

Romans 16:25–27

In another passage Paul elaborates even further that his stewardship involved the "preaching of the word of God, that is, the mystery which has been hidden from the past ages and generations" (Col.

103

1:25–26). He later wrote to Timothy of the mystery of godliness as "He who was revealed in the flesh, was vindicated in the Spirit, seen by angels, proclaimed among the nations, believed on in the world, taken up in glory" (1 Tim. 3:16).

The disciples were to steward the gospel faithfully, and the under-shepherds of Christ who pastor churches today have inherited this stewardship. The word *required* (*zeteo*) is very strong and would be better translated "demanded" in 1 Corinthians 4:2: It is demanded of stewards that they be faithful in managing the gospel of Christ. Preaching is a primary act in the ministry of Christ's under-shepherds. A lack of biblical preaching is often an obvious sign of the impending death of a church. As God's stewards of the Word of God, pastors must handle it with care (2 Cor. 2:17). They should be diligent to present themselves approved to God as workmen who do not need to be ashamed, "accurately handling the word of truth" (2 Tim. 2:15). A faithful steward from past years says it well: "The business of a steward is not to electrify people by his eloquent sermons, not to dazzle them by flowers of rhetoric . . . but the business of a servant of Christ is to open up the truth of God, to unfold, to expound, to make known these mysteries."[9]

Faithful preaching is needed for biblical church growth, but stewardship requires more than handling the Word of God well. It also implies a responsibility for leading God's people to take the mystery of Christ to all nations. A full understanding of faithful stewardship recognizes there is a coming day of accountability. Often stewards were given responsibility for their master's household, and they were accountable for using those assets well.

Christ communicated that a time is coming when servants will be held accountable for their stewardship. In the parable of the talents (Matt. 25:14–30), Christ told of three stewards who were given money to invest for their master. One was given five talents, another two, and the last steward one talent. The stewards who had been given five talents and two talents immediately invested them and doubled their master's money. Unfortunately, the last steward was too fearful to risk losing his master's money and hid it in the ground. After some time went by, the master returned and called his stewards to account. The first two stewards stepped forward and reported that they had doubled their master's investments. To each he said, "Well done, good and faithful slave. You were faithful with a few things, I will put you in charge of many things; enter into the joy of your master"(vv. 21, 23). The last steward came and told the master that he was afraid of him, so he returned the master's investment without any increase. The master was angry and called his servant a "wicked, lazy slave" (v. 26). The point of the parable is that the master will hold his stewards accountable, and it is important to note that the faithful stewards were the ones who increased their master's investment (see also Luke 16:1–13).

God has not called pastors to be successful in an earthly sense but to be faithful. We should not deceive ourselves, however; faithfulness requires more than simply holding down the fort. The bottom line of faithful leadership is biblical church growth, that is, the actual increase in countable disciples and the number of new churches planted. Donald McGavran expressed it this way:

> Can the quarter-back or captain advance the ball down the field? We answer, "That is his principle function. He administers the team so that the ball advances, yards are gained, and points scored. . . . He knows that his success is not going to be measured by the skill with which he keeps the team moving, the precision of his plays, or the goodwill of his players. It is going to be measured by touchdowns and field goals."[10]

Pastoral leadership cannot just be concerned with the spiritual growth of the members, important as that is, but also must be concerned with the spread of the gospel message to all nations. A faithful pastor lives a life of purity and righteousness and leads his flock to do its part in fulfilling the Great Commission. A faithful pastor not only instills a vision of growth in his people but also makes sure that structures are in place to make biblical growth possible.

Our Savior God, keep us focused most closely on carrying out the Great Commission. This is the task to which You have called us, that rivers of the water of life might flow freely throughout the parched and

thirsty land. Deliver us from all easy irresponsibility, all mouthing of platitudes regardless of the actual extent of the spread of the churches. May we hunger and thirst after effectiveness in our missionary activity. May we constantly reach out to become better servants of You, who came to seek and save the lost, more closely identified with You, who gave Your life a ransom for many, more ready to give our accounts, Lord, to You, when it pleases You to call us home.

Donald A. McGavran[11]

Questions to Ask and Answer

1. Is Jesus the Chief Shepherd of your church? Point out some practical ways your church looks to Jesus for leadership.
2. To what extent do the pastors of your church equip others to do the work of ministry? To what extent do they tend to do the work themselves?
3. How do your pastors and church leaders balance character and competence?
4. What is your understanding of the concept of being a faithful shepherd? How does it fit with the role of a steward?
5. Who does the pathfinding in your church? How is the mission of your church determined and communicated?

EIGHT

The Right People

Effective Ministers

> If a church is serious about the Great Commission, the involvement of the laity is of utmost importance. The growth of each church is uniquely dependent on its laity.
>
> Donald McGavran and Win Arn

A good friend of mine pastored a church that had grown significantly during his first three years of ministry. He was an excellent strategist who effectively developed a plan for growth, rallied church members behind it, and executed the plan flawlessly. It appeared that all was in place for continued growth. During the fourth year of his ministry, however, attendance began falling noticeably, and the church never reached its potential. The reason, at least in part, was the congregation's unwillingness to cooperate with God in the growth of his church.

The members' unwillingness to serve one another first became obvious in the children's ministry. Attendance at the traditional evening worship service had been declining, so the church leaders started a new Sunday evening Bible institute modeled after a local community college's evening adult classes. This new approach to Christian education worked well until problems arose with child care. As it turned out, few people were willing to invest their time and gifts in caring for the children while other adults attended the evening classes. Several creative options for providing child care were attempted, but no matter what approach was used, people were just unwilling to serve in the children's area of ministry. After months of frustrated efforts, the church leaders were forced to cancel the Bible institute, crippling the church's ability to provide training for its people.

About a year later a similar attitude surfaced among those who served in the music ministry of the church. One reason for the rapid growth during those first three years was the addition of a second worship service. It took extra energy by the members of the music ministry to provide a vibrant worship experience for two services rather than one. But they were more than willing—at first—to minister in this way if new people were being assimilated into their church. All went well for a couple of years. Then, toward the end of the third year, members of the worship team complained that they were feeling worn out from the rigors of leading two services. It was suggested that a second worship team be recruited and deployed in ministry to offer relief to the first team. Unfortunately, the leaders of the music ministry felt that adding a second team would be insulting to the original team members who had volunteered so faithfully for three years. Unable to come up with a workable solution, and with the discouragement of the worship team increasing, the leadership decided to revert to a single worship service. The first Sunday when there was only one worship service, attendance was down by 15 percent. It never recovered.

The people's lack of commitment expressed itself in other ways. As the church grew, the facilities and parking lot became overcrowded to the point that newcomers could no longer fit. When an opportunity came to buy land bordering the church property that would allow for expansion of the church's parking lot, the leaders took the initiative to move forward in faith to purchase the land. Unfortunately, as you might have guessed, when the opportunity was presented to the congregation, it was voted down.

Growing People

The truth is that *growing people grow churches*. Numerical growth can occur in a local church for a time due to outside factors, but such growth will not last unless the people reached also grow spiritually. Biblical church growth takes place when there is a balance between numerical growth and spiritual growth.

The Great Commission illustrates this balance in the use of the words *go, baptize,* and *teach.* As a church goes out to evangelize the lost and then effectively assimilates new converts into the life of the church, it experiences numerical growth. In an overlapping manner, as a church embraces the new converts into fellowship and teaches them to observe all that Christ commanded, spiritual growth takes place. The overlapping nature of numerical growth and spiritual growth is illustrated below.

Make Disciples

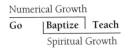

Unfortunately, many churches fall into a trap of viewing spiritual growth as simply a matter of nurturing the development of spiritual disciplines, such as Bible reading, prayer, and worship. It's true that spiritual growth means developing one's walk with the Lord, for which these disciplines are crucial, yet spiritual growth was never intended to be self-centered.

A focus on spiritual maturity as an end in itself always creates a self-centered church. Spiritual growth does not mean that people grow just in their knowledge of the Bible, their prayer lives, or their worship. There are numerous churches wherein people are nurtured in biblical knowledge but do not use their knowledge in ministry to others. Such "nurture-oriented education commits the serious error of making an end of something that is meant to be a means. . . . By definition it [nurture-oriented education] is self-centered and therefore suffers from a basic introversion."[1] Writing about the important spiritual elements of wor-

The Right People—Effective Ministers

Life-giving churches are empowered by worshipers who willingly invest their lives in life-giving ministry.

ship and prayer, C. Peter Wagner states, "They are divinely appointed means to prepare and equip us for the central task of fulfilling the Great Commission. God wants His Kingdom to come to earth. He wants lost people saved. He wants cities and nations transformed."[2]

A biblically growing church remembers that God promised to bless Abraham so that he would be a blessing (see Gen. 12:2). A church that grows spiritually must of necessity reach out to bless others, or we could question whether its people are really growing spiritually. True spiritual growth means that people move away from a self-centered attitude and reach out in ministry to others. The apostle Peter said, "As each one has received a special gift, employ it in serving one another as good stewards of the manifold grace of God" (1 Peter 4:10).

Growing people demonstrate a ministry mind-set, which is seen in the light of the Great Commission. Thus the sixth principle for biblical church growth is that a church must have the *right people:* effective ministers. Simply stated, *life-giving churches are empowered by worshipers who willingly invest their lives in life-giving ministry.*

There is a difference between growing a crowd and growing a church. To be effective leaders, pastors must decide to *make* ministers rather than simply *be* a minister. They must see themselves as the coach of the team rather than the owner of the team. Rather than seeking to build programs, they must focus on building people. The apostle Paul reminds us that church leaders are not to do all the work but are to equip "the saints for the work of service, to the building up of the body of Christ" (Eph. 4:12). It may help to visualize this equipping function of the pastors this way:

110

Equipping (katartismos) means "to repair or mend." It is the word from which we get "artist" or "craftsman," and it refers to crafting or mending something with one's hands. It carries the idea of preparing a person to be fully ready to do a job. The concept is that the pastor of a church is not to do the ministry alone but is to craft and mend others, preparing them for ministry.

The reason pastors are to equip others to do ministry is that the greatest resource in a church is its people—not the programs or facilities or finances. "People win people. Programs do not reach people; people reach people."[3] Biblical church growth occurs only as people are deployed in effective ministry, as illustrated below.

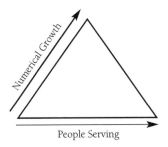

Viewed as a pyramid, the growth of a church is obviously dependent on people who are willing to serve each other with their gifts. As more and more people are added to a church, there is a parallel need for more people to serve in support of the total body. If a church grows numerically but its people do not grow spiritually and become involved in ministry, the church will eventually reach a breaking point when the people supporting the ministry become overburdened. As a result church growth will cease.

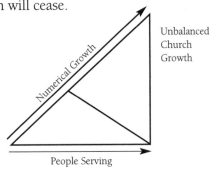

In churches that experience biblical church growth, people are constantly trained and released to use their spiritual gifts in service to others. As a balance between the numerical growth and spiritual growth of the church is reached and maintained, the church experiences biblical church growth.

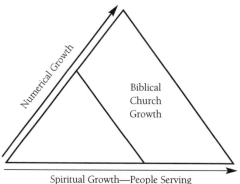

Spiritual Growth—People Serving

Churches normally experience growth as they involve more of their members in an identifiable ministry. A church with 27 percent or less of its people involved in an identifiable ministry role is usually in decline. A church with 28 to 54 percent involved is often on a plateau. A church with 55 percent or more of its people serving in ministry is usually growing. However, the percentage of people involved in ministry is only part of a more intricate principle, as discussed below.

The ratio of volunteers to consumers in a church tells a lot about the church's health. For the purpose of understanding the larger picture, it is helpful to think of people as consumers, internal volunteers, or external volunteers. Consumers are members who do not serve in the church for whatever reason. Some people may not be able to serve due to age or illness. Others may work long hours that keep them from serving on a regular time schedule. A few will decline to serve due to a negative experience at church. They consume the ministry of others without giving much back in service to others.

Internal volunteers become involved in roles that serve the existing church. They serve as ushers, greeters, nursery workers, Sunday school teachers, cooks, church secretaries, and in a host of other positions. It would be hard for a church to get along without them.

Smart Move

Do some research to find out exactly how many people in your church are actually serving in identifiable ministry positions. Determine how many of those who are serving are internal volunteers and external volunteers. Then draw a graph similar to the ones below showing the total number of consumers, internal volunteers, and external volunteers. Which church does yours most closely resemble? Is it a growing, plateaued, or declining church?

External volunteers focus their efforts on serving people outside the existing church. They actively serve in ministries that seek to win people to Christ by leading Bible studies, distributing evangelistic literature, organizing evangelistic teams, leading small groups, directing 12-step programs, and doing a variety of other outwardly focused ministries.

The more consumers a church has, the less likely it is to grow. The more volunteers there are in a church, the more opportunity there is for growth. And as more volunteers find their way into external ministry roles, a church finds even more possibility for growth. Note the following examples. If a church has fewer than 27 percent of its people serving in ministry roles, the result is a large number of consumers who absorb a significant amount of energy from the small number of volunteers. A church in this situation usually finds itself in decline with limited potential for growth.

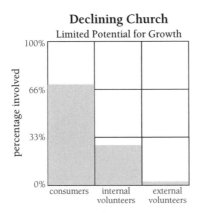

Declining Church
Limited Potential for Growth

A church with about 43 percent of its members involved is usually on a plateau. Those who are serving find themselves primarily working internally to serve the still large number of consumers.

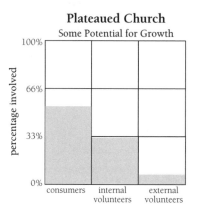

Plateaued Church

When a church sees more than 55 percent of its people using their gifts in ministry, it begins to grow. The smaller number of consumers allows a larger number of volunteers to serve in external ministries.

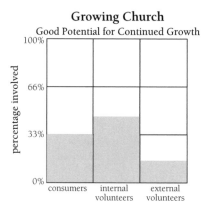

Growing Church

The Modus Operandi

The life-giving Spirit empowers people for ministry, and his modus operandi is to give spiritual gifts to believers. Two main words are used for spiritual gifts in the Bible. The first is a combination of two parts: *pneuma* meaning "spirit" and *ikon* meaning "things concerning." The word means "something that belongs to the spiritual realm." Paul uses this word when he writes, "Now concerning spiritual gifts, brethren, I do not want you to be unaware" (1 Cor. 12:1; see also 14:1). The most frequently used word for spiritual gifts is *charisma,* which is derived from *charis,* which means "grace." A spiritual gift is something all believers receive from God as part of his grace (see Rom. 12:3; 1 Peter 4:10). It is used in reference to God's gift of salvation (Rom. 5:15–16; 6:23), of kindness shown to others (Rom. 1:11; 2 Cor. 1:11), and of a special ability for service (Rom. 12:6; 1 Cor. 1:7; 12:4; 1 Peter 4:10).

Spiritual gifts are a part of every believer's spiritual inheritance since they have been blessed with all spiritual blessings (Eph. 1:3) and have obtained an inheritance with Christ (v. 11). God is the source of spiritual gifts, and all three members of the Godhead are involved in the giving of spiritual gifts to the body, as seen in Paul's introductory comment on spiritual gifts: "Now there are varieties of gifts, but the same Spirit. And there are varieties of ministries, and the same Lord. There are varieties of effects, but the same God who works in all things in all persons" (1 Cor. 12:4–6). However, the Holy Spirit has a special role in the dispersing of spiritual gifts. Paul writes, "But to each one is given the manifestation of the Spirit for the common good. For to one is given the word of wisdom through the Spirit, and to another the word of knowledge according to the same Spirit; to another faith by the same Spirit, and to another gifts of healing by the one Spirit. . . . But one and the same Spirit works all these things, distributing to each one individually just as He wills" (1 Cor. 12:7–11).

Each believer has at least one spiritual gift, for God has "allotted to each a measure of faith" (Rom. 12:3), and "each has received a special gift" (1 Peter 4:10). The gifts are task-oriented and congregational. They are task-oriented in that they are given not primarily for a person's own spiritual growth but to serve others (see Rom. 12:6–13). They are congregational in that they are primarily to be used to serve others within the context of the church, as the metaphor of the body teaches (1 Cor. 12:14–26). In the majority of cases, the use of gifts will be exercised in local congregations where people meet to encourage one another (Heb. 10:25).

Spiritual gifts are to be used in submission to the will of God. It is no accident that Paul begins his discourse on spiritual gifts in Romans

12 with verses one and two: "I urge you, brethren, by the mercies of God, to present your bodies a living and holy sacrifice, acceptable to God, which is your spiritual service of worship. And do not be conformed to this world, but be transformed by the renewing of your mind, so that you may prove what the will of God is, that which is good and acceptable and perfect." It is easy for spiritual gifts to be used in a selfish manner as happened in Corinth. This church did not lack any gifts (1 Cor. 1:7), but their selfish use of them created quarrels and divisions in the church. For believers to be effective in their use of their spiritual gifts, they must consecrate themselves to God and use their gifts for the benefit of others.

Observation of growing churches reveals that it is not the different understandings of spiritual gifts that cause a church to grow or decline, but it is the use or lack of use of spiritual gifts that makes the difference. For example, some churches that believe sign gifts are for use today are growing. However, other churches that do not believe sign gifts are appropriate for use today are also growing. It is the willingness of the people to serve or not to serve that makes the difference.

Growing churches believe:

1. All gifts are needed in the body of Christ (1 Cor. 12:14–26).
2. Every member of a local church has a unique function that is important to the well-being of the whole body (v. 17).
3. Spiritual gifts are diverse (v. 4).
4. Each church must determine its own understanding of which spiritual gifts are proper for their use (Rom. 12:3).

Spiritually mature people understand that there is no greater calling in life than to serve one another with the gifts God has given them. It was the model of all that Christ did (Mark 10:43–45; Luke 22:24–27). It is part of our worship (Col. 3:1–2), our attitude (Matt. 6:24), and our lifestyle (Eph. 4:14–16).

Elements for Service

To develop an effective lay ministry so that biblical church growth can take place, a church must commit to four key elements. First, *peo-*

ple must know and buy into the church's vision. People commit to vision. If people are not getting involved in ministry, it is a good indication that the vision of the church is not well-known. A pastor or leadership board may develop and communicate a vision for the church, but if the members do not feel it is their vision, they will rarely have the "fire in the belly" to support it, going up against impossible odds and taking impossible risks for the sake of the gospel. It is imperative that church leaders be clear about the church's vision and be able to articulate it to others in ways that create ownership among the members.

Closely attached to identification with the vision is the opportunity to do something of significance. For many years churches relied on volunteers to do simple tasks, such as licking postage stamps, preparing meals, and making phone calls to shut-ins. Today similar tasks need to be accomplished, but often volunteers are looking to become involved in more challenging venues. The attitude of today's volunteers is, *Let us do some of the challenging things, and let's hire people to do the routine work.* Growing churches talk up the job of ministry, and their people rise to the challenge. People want to be involved in something that is meaningful.

Second, *people must have a biblical view of ministry and service to be motivated.* Spiritual gifts are for ministry rather than maintenance. They are for the growth of the church rather than the inreach of the church. People need to realize that their ministry is ultimately a spiritual task to serve others that will also bring them meaning. Involvement in ministry provides a source of community and a way to improve their own lives. Most of all, people need to believe that what they are doing is important. Whatever their eventual role, it needs to be seen as part of the work of God's kingdom.

Church leaders may get discouraged and feel that people are not willing to serve the Lord and his church, but there really is no shortage of talented people. There are plenty of them in our churches. It is just that people have a great deal of competition for their time. Church members use their time coaching youth sports, working in their yards, boating at the lake, and many other endeavors. Like some observant person noted: We all have time to do what we want to do. The burden is on church leaders to become more rigorous and creative in finding the talent they need and convincing those people to become

117

F.Y.I.

Today's volunteers want to have a ministry description. They desire to know where their role begins and ends. Having a ministry description is often the first indication that a church expects a high level of commitment from its volunteers and that it intends to select them carefully and with respect. A signed agreement is a good way to cement commitment.

---

involved. In times gone by people gave priority time to their church, but that is not so today. People prioritize their time based on the perceived value of its use. When they understand the value of their gifts and how they can impact others, they will be willing to serve.

Third, *the church must have a workable system to help people identify and use their spiritual gifts.* The local church is one of the most difficult organizations to lead due to the fact that the people in it are volunteers, and the church must care for the same people it uses in ministry. Most organizations do not have to provide care for those who work or serve with them. Such care is provided through other means or organizations. This puts a church in a situation in which it must take a somewhat sophisticated approach to recruiting, training, and motivating workers.

Like all people, church volunteers need leadership. They need to be recruited, trained, motivated, and deployed in ministry. They need to be provided with adequate resources and the necessary tools to do their ministry. Churches that experience biblical church growth systematically recruit, train, and deploy members in ministry. Declining churches rarely have any defined system to identify potential volunteers, assess their giftedness, and place them in appropriate ministry positions.

Fourth, *growing churches involve people early on in ministry.* When Paul planted churches, he involved people in ministry quickly. Many times the people were inexperienced, but they were energetic and willing to serve. He did not wait to involve them, because then their interest may have waned to the point of noninterest. Unless people become involved in ministry within three to six months after they first attend church on a regular basis, they may never become involved.

The mobilization of people to participate in direct service to each other and the world is a major ingredient in biblical church growth. The early church, described in Acts, grew not because growth was easy but because men and women committed themselves to sacrificial service to each other and to lost people. Filled with intense conviction, the power of the Holy Spirit, and love for God, ordinary men and women overcame tremendous obstacles to tell others about the Savior. Churches that effectively recruit, train, and deploy their people in faithful ministry will find they too have tremendous potential for biblical church growth.

We thank You, Lord our God, for the revelation of yourself—God of righteousness and mercy. We pray that You will give grace to walk in the light You have revealed and to obey your commands and to feed on your Word. And, Lord, we ask that your church everywhere may turn from error and from sin and become faithful followers of your Son and responsible members of His Body. In Christ's name we pray. Amen.

Donald A. McGavran[4]

Questions to Ask and Answer

1. What has been the history of lay ministry in your church? Has it been positive or negative?
2. Does your church have a systematic way to recruit, train, and deploy volunteer workers in ministry? Is it effective?
3. Has your church developed a clear statement of its purpose, values, and vision? Does the congregation understand this statement, believe it, and own the stated purpose, values, and vision?

4. What is your church's understanding of spiritual gifts? Are people encouraged to develop their gifts and use them in ministry? Why or why not?

5. How soon are newcomers encouraged to become involved in some form of service or ministry? Can you identify entry-level ministry roles in which new people are asked to become involved?

NINE

The Right Philosophy
Cultural Relevance

> The true goal is to multiply, in every piece of the magnificent mosaic, truly Christian churches which fit that piece, are closely adapted to its culture, and recognized by its non-Christians as "our kind of show."
>
> Donald A. McGavran

My wife and I recently visited a church in California that took us back in time. When we entered the lobby of the church building, we heard piano music coming from the sanctuary. The music was that of a familiar Fanny Crosby hymn played in a very distinctive style that dated back to about the mid-nineteenth century. As we walked toward the doors leading into the sanctuary, I leaned over to my wife and whispered, "Youth for Christ—1945."

After we took our seats in the sanctuary, I noticed that everyone in the church was dressed in their Sunday best. Now, I am not against dressing up to go to church. In fact I personally prefer wearing a suit and tie on Sunday. Yet it seemed out of place in our day and age to see everyone—and I mean everyone—dressed up. Even the elementary school boys were wearing suits and ties, and each little girl had on a frilly dress. Many ladies wore dressy hats, and every man had on a tie.

When the pastor began to preach, he spoke with a tone of voice that sounded like a recording of classical oratory common to the late 1800s. As the message progressed, the pastor moved down to the floor, removed his suit coat, and gradually walked closer to where we were sitting, until he stood about ten pews in front of us. Beginning his closing invitation, the pastor glanced sternly toward us and warned of a coming condemnation. Our entire worship experience felt like we were stuck in a time-warp purgatory.

No doubt the people and pastor meant well. It's sad, however, that this church is so culturally out of touch with the community that it has limited impact for Christ. Like many churches, this one has made the mistake of confusing culture with core values. The members believe that their way of dressing for worship is right and other forms of dress are wrong. They communicate that their choice of music is correct and others are not acceptable. Even the cars in their parking lot shouted loudly that only automobiles made in our country are proper for Christians to drive. They mix Christian tastes with biblical values and create barriers between people and Christ.

Churches tend to approach culture from one of three perspectives— isolation, domination, or incarnation. Isolation takes place when a church, such as the one we visited, is so far removed from culture that it can no longer communicate the Good News in effective ways. If isolation takes over completely, it usually causes a church to die. However, most cases of isolation simply result in a church that has limited impact on people in the community and society.

Domination occurs as a church lashes out harshly against the perceived evils of culture. While churches using this approach to culture occasionally play the part of prophet, in the majority of situations, they are just ignored as part of the fanatical fringe.

Observation of churches throughout history demonstrates that the best approach to making disciples is incarnational. Martin Luther used this approach when he wrote new lyrics to the traditional tunes of his day, tunes that were sung in the bars and taverns. John Wesley followed this path when he began speaking the gospel directly to the miners of England and gathered them into small groups that met in

The Right Philosophy—Cultural Relevance

Life-giving churches relate to their communities
in culturally relevant ways.

homes rather than in cathedrals. Both Luther and Wesley appropriately adapted to the cultural setting of their day.

Incarnation happens when a church adapts itself in appropriate ways to its culture so that the culture will receive a hearing of the gospel. Jesus told us to be fishers of men (Matt. 4:19; Mark 1:17). Churches that isolate themselves from the culture do not fish. Those that seek to dominate the culture fish with dynamite. Churches that incarnate themselves into the culture fish with the proper bait and tackle.

Biblical church growth takes place in churches that are indigenous to their mission field. They customize their worship, teaching, outreach, and ministries to their specific cultural and demographic settings by following the *right philosophy:* cultural relevance. Simply stated, *life-giving churches relate to their communities in culturally relevant ways.*

A Short History of Culture

It is clear that the many cultures of the world had their roots in the life-giving God. All of the endless varieties of human life, work, language, and vocations find their source in the creativeness of the Godhead. It seems evident that if Adam had not sinned, he and Eve would have had numerous children, and eventually distinct cultural groups would have developed, displaying the abundant variety of God's nature. Such a proliferation of cultures would have developed within a sinless environment. However, since Adam sinned, all cultures of the world have been infected by sin and include immoral aspects. Although culture is sourced in God, he is not involved in the development of its immoral aspects, since he "cannot be tempted by evil, and He Himself does not tempt anyone" (James 1:13).

The first indication of different cultures appears in Genesis, where we are told, "Abel was a keeper of flocks, but Cain was a tiller of the ground" (4:2). The different roles or jobs would have caused uniquely different cultures to develop around each of these men. Even today we can observe distinct cultural milieus around shepherds and farmers. Genesis also tells us that the families of Cain continued to develop special roles, such as ranchers (v. 20), musicians (v. 21), and miners (v. 22). It is instructive that the Bible says nothing negative about this behavior. In fact it is a legitimate behavior of people, and no doubt the families of Cain's sons gradually developed special customs, traditions, and values associated with these vocations—they developed culture.

Following the flood, the sons of Noah began to spread out and develop distinct cultures wherever they settled (10:2–32). The unifying factor was their language, which led them to disobey God's command to repopulate the earth. "They said, 'Come, let us build for ourselves a city, and a tower whose top will reach into heaven, and let us make for ourselves a name, otherwise we will be scattered abroad over the face of the whole earth'" (11:4).

Rather than allow the people to remain together with one language, in one location, and perhaps with one false religion, God decided to "confuse their language" so they would not understand each other's speech and would be scattered over the whole earth (vv. 7–9). This act alone accelerated the growth of cultures throughout the world. It must be pointed out that the development of varied cultures was within God's will. It is highly probable that the mosaic of cultures we now see in our world would have developed even as people from one tribe, community, or family went their separate ways. When God confused their languages, diversity just happened at a faster pace.

Charles Kraft writes, "Culture is not in and of itself either an enemy or friend to God or humans. It is, rather, something that is there to be used by personal beings such as humans, God, and Satan."[1] Basically, culture is the symbols, rites, values, customs, language, and idioms that are transferred from one generation to another. It is the manner of thinking and perceiving that a group of people has in common. Such aspects of cultural heritage are owned by a specific group of people in a specific location at a specific time in history.

From Canaan to Africa

Some people make the mistake of thinking that Christianity can be contained in a specific true culture, usually defined as the original culture in which they were raised or first received the gospel. Unfortunately, holding on to the idea of a "true culture" does not make for effective disciple making.

A close look at the Bible reveals that there is no single true culture or way of life. In truth it appears that God delights in moving people out of one culture into a new one. For example, in the Old Testament the people of God moved from Ur to Canaan (Gen. 12:1–5) to Egypt (Genesis 46) to Babylon (Dan. 1:1–7) and back. Each move forced them to decide what was core to their beliefs and values and what was not. In the New Testament God continued to press the early church out of its comfortable cultural surroundings. The church moved from Jerusalem (Acts 1) to Samaria (Acts 8:1–24) to Ethiopia (vv. 25–40) to Antioch, Phoenicia, and Cyprus (11:19–20) and on to the ends of the world (1:8).

What was God's purpose in moving his people from culture to culture? It appears that he wanted them to carry their faith to different peoples and to learn how to communicate in different cultural forms. Disciples can be made in all the nations (*panta ta ethne*) but only if the gospel message is communicated within each specific culture. Every tribe, people, family, or ethnic group has its own culture and numerous subcultures, so there is much need for adaptation. While the gospel message remains the same, its communication must be uniquely tailored for each specific cultural group if it is to be heard and believed. One observer of the missionary movement in North America writes, "Spreading the gospel is becoming less and less a geographical problem. Increasingly it is a cultural challenge. There are few places where the church has not gone. But, there are many groups of people who have not heard the gospel in *ways that attract their attention.*"[2]

We can be certain that God did not want his people to preserve a particular cultural way of life as a "true culture." A culture is relevant in a given location for a limited time. No culture can be universally relevant. So churches must adapt appropriately to the indigenous cultures in which they reside. Those that do so tend to enjoy biblical church growth.

The key to this growth is that churches adapt *appropriately*. A church must relate to its culture, not be shaped by it. Every identifiable culture has its good and bad elements, and the Bible stands in judgment over every human cultural form and tradition. Any time a church interfaces with culture, there is the potential that it will be absorbed by the secular, so churches must hold themselves to a standard of style and a level of practice that are culturally relevant and doctrinally pure. To adapt to the culture never means compromising the faith and standards of the gospel. Elmer Towns writes, "This does not mean we change eternal ministry principles based on the Word of God. But it does mean we use old-fashioned principles in a contemporary manner."[3] The lifestyle of a church must please the Lord, yet in small matters it should not be so shockingly different from those among whom it ministers as to make unintelligible the message it wishes to convey. Thus churches must wisely select which cultural forms may be adopted and adapted, as well as which forms must be avoided. It takes wisdom to make certain that a ministry is not being "conformed to this world" (Rom. 12:2) and that those who are ministering are relating to lost people in ways they can understand and believe. It is crucial to faithful ministry to recognize that Christ did not pull his church out of the world; rather he sent his church into the world to make an impact on it (John 17:13–19). It is not always an easy balance to maintain, but it is possible.

Culture and subcultures are observed in various tribes, families, peoples, or ethnic groups (*ethne,* see Matt. 28:19–20). To reach them, "the forms of outreach, ministry, and worship must be indigenous to their culture, because each people's culture is the natural medium of God's revelation to them."[4] God, of course, knew this, and so when his Son came to earth, he adopted the culture in which he lived and ministered.

Adapting to Culture

Jesus set the example for incarnation as he "became flesh, and dwelt among us" (John 1:14). The word *dwelt* means to "pitch a tent" (*skenoo*).

A *tent* is often used figuratively for the body. In this verse, it means that Christ came to be a part of humanity; that is, he took on human form and lived as a man. The human form he tented in was in a particular time and place among a peculiar people and culture, as the genealogy of Matthew 1:1–17 so carefully documents. Jesus was a "descendant of David according to the flesh" (Rom. 1:3). Adapting to his culture, Jesus spoke in the languages and communication patterns of his time, used illustrations and stories that were understood by people of his culture, ate the food appropriate to his people, observed the customs of his family, and wore the dress of his contemporaries. To do otherwise would have been ludicrous as well as ineffective.

Being in the flesh, Jesus was able to identify with those he came to save. He became hungry (Matt. 4:2) and was able to "sympathize with our weaknesses," being "tempted in all things as we are, yet without sin" (Heb. 4:15). Most important, since we are "flesh and blood, He Himself likewise also partook of the same, that through death He might render powerless him who had the power of death, that is, the devil" (2:14).

Jesus engaged in his culture by understanding it and selecting approaches that communicated effectively with people in its various segments. For example, Jesus ministered to Nicodemus (John 3) and the Samaritan woman (John 4) in two distinct ways. Culturally, Nicodemus was an elite Jew with formal training as a Pharisee. As an inquisitive, self-righteous teacher, he sought Jesus to ask him questions. The Samaritan woman was culturally a lower-class God-fearer with an informal education. Having lived a life of sin, she was indifferent to Jesus, even surprised he would talk with her.

Jesus carefully selected a unique approach to each one—an approach calculated to penetrate their specific cultural backgrounds. Jesus spoke to Nicodemus in a formal, private setting. Their conversation centered around spiritual matters on the theme of being born again. Jesus revealed himself as the Son of Man and a master teacher. His basic approach was to use an abstract theological discussion. As they concluded their conversation, Jesus offered spiritual birth to Nicodemus if he would believe.

When Jesus spoke with the Samaritan woman, he used a different approach, one that was very concrete and personal. He had a casual

---

Smart Move

On a blank sheet of paper list all the ministries and programs that your church conducted in the last month. Beside each one put the date in which the ministry was originally started. How many of the ministries were started within the last year? The last five years? The last ten years? What does this say about your church's willingness to adapt appropriately to the culture?

---

conversation with her in a public place and spoke of physical matters, such as water and husbands. Jesus revealed himself as the Messiah and a prophet. As they concluded their conversation, Jesus offered the woman living water. In both cases Jesus adapted his communication to his audience, but he did not change his message.

The apostle Paul was culturally a Jew, but God called him to reach a variety of people called Gentiles (Gal. 1:15–16). This required him to adapt his presentation of the gospel to different cultural and subcultural groups. Yet he continued to "preach Christ crucified, to Jews a stumbling block and to Gentiles foolishness" (1 Cor. 1:23). Paul changed his approach but not his message.

An example of how Paul adjusted his style to reach a variety of cultures is revealed in Acts 17. While they were all part of the Roman Empire, the people of Thessalonica, Berea, and Athens were culturally different. Each group had distinct attitudes, customs, values, symbols, and idioms. Paul met and adapted to a new set of cultural circumstances in each city, approaching the people in defined ways.

Thessalonica was a major trade center composed of Hellenistic Jews and God-fearing and secular Gentiles. Because of the wealth that had come to the city, the people were extremely materialistic and protective of their trade (see Acts 17:5–9). They tended to react strongly against anything or anyone that threatened their standard view of the world.

Berea was a small town out of the way of the major trade routes. The citizenry was predominantly orthodox Jews and God-fearing Gentiles. They had developed much more of a fair-minded, open, and accommodating value system than found in Thessalonica (see vv. 11–15).

Athens was a large metropolis and cultural center made up of people who were idolaters, many being superstitious and philosophic idealists. They had great civic pride and were cynical and skeptical of other belief systems (see vv. 18–32).

Paul correctly perceived that the people in each city needed to be approached in a slightly different way for him to get a hearing for the gospel. He confronted the Thessalonians directly, demonstrating that Christ was the suffering and risen Messiah (v. 3). Because the Bereans were eager to learn and would patiently investigate what he had to say, Paul approached them in a consultative manner to demonstrate that Jesus was the fulfillment of the Old Testament Scriptures (v. 11). As a people, the Athenians were skeptics who were difficult to convince about the truth of the gospel. Fortunately, Paul observed that they were also curious, which gave him a door of opportunity to preach the Good News. Adopting the philosophical approach so loved by the Athenians, Paul engaged them in dialogue to show that Jesus was the unknown God, Creator, Judge, and resurrected Man (vv. 23–32).[5]

The responses to Paul's messages varied greatly, with most of the fruit coming from Thessalonica (v. 4) and Berea (v. 12), and only a little from Athens (v. 34). Presenting the gospel in a culturally relevant manner does not guarantee that people will believe or that a church will grow. Yet doing so follows the model established by Christ and his servant Paul. Following their model, a church that desires to grow biblically will incarnate the gospel message in the style, language, aesthetics, and music of the people it is seeking to win to Christ. In effect it will become a missional church, that is, understanding and adapting to a culture like a missionary does in another land.

Today's world continues to be a rich mosaic of cultures. While some cultures and subcultures are disappearing, there still exist thousands of different cultural expressions to which the gospel message must be adapted. As Donald McGavran reminded us some years ago: "The true goal is to multiply, in every piece of the magnificent mosaic, truly Christian churches which fit that piece, are closely adapted to its culture, and are recognized by its non-Christians as 'our kind of show.'"[6]

Another Smart Move

During the next month, carefully keep note of the songs used in your worship services. Make a list of each song and note its copyright date beside it. After one month, rewrite your list of songs beginning with the one with the newest copyright down to the one with the oldest copyright. What does the music of your church indicate about your church's ability to adapt in appropriate ways to culture? Are you using any music that was written in the last five years? Ten years? What cultural era does most of your music reflect?

Using New Tools

Biblical church growth emphasizes Christ, not culture. God is not bound to any one culture but is transcultural. In his book *How to Reach Secular People,* George Hunter says, "Christianity everywhere is rooted in 'the same gospel' and is, in fact, the one demonstrated 'universal faith,' but it must be contextualized for every people and culture."[7]

The different cultures and subcultures represented among the people of the world contain morally neutral and immoral aspects. Those parts of culture that are morally neutral are avenues where God works to demonstrate his glory. Those areas that are immoral are ones that need transformation through the power of the gospel.

The apostle Paul depicts his approach to culture in this way:

> For though I am free from all men, I have made myself a slave to all, so that I may win more. To the Jews I became as a Jew, so that I might win Jews; to those who are under the Law, as under the Law though not being myself under the Law, so that I might win those who are under the Law; to those who are without law, as without law, though not being without the law of God but under the law of Christ, so that I might win those who are without law. To the weak I became weak, that I might win the weak; I have become all things to all men, so that I may by all means save some. I do all things for the sake of the gospel, so that I may become a fellow partaker of it.
>
> 1 Corinthians 9:19–23

It is striking that Paul uses the phrase "that I might win" or "that I may win" five times in this brief passage and once says, "that I may by all means save some." It was his goal to communicate the gospel so that as many people as possible might be saved. How did he do this? By becoming a slave to all; that is, he limited his own cultural practices and preferences so that he would not be a barrier between unbelievers and Christ. It was Paul's act of love, a voluntary slavery, to reach others by being willing to abide by the laws and customs of the Jews, the Gentiles, or any people who lacked knowledge of the gospel. He crafted his presentation, lifestyle, and methods to a particular people and their cultural ability to comprehend the gospel. He drew a careful distinction in noting that he was under the law of Christ. Paul was willing to accommodate himself to a culture but only if he could do it without going against the direct teachings of Christ or God's moral law. Yet in other nonmoral issues he would adapt as much as he needed to so that he "might win" some to Christ. Paul was willing to use all means (pantos), whatever he could do that was morally acceptable, to bring others to Christ.

> As the culture changes and people manifest different needs, the church must update its techniques to accomplish the goal.
>
> Elmer Towns[8]

Christian lifestyles create separation between people, as Jesus warned. Some people in our modern culture prefer sin—deceit, greed, and lust—and rightly ought to feel dissidence between their choices and the Christian way of life. However, not all aspects of culture are evil. Some practices are strictly related to one's preference or time in history. They really fall into the realm of tradition and cultural values rather than biblical truths and eternal values. When a church is biblically sensitive, as Paul was, to "please all men in all things, not seeking my own profit but the profit of the many, so that they may be saved" (1 Cor. 10:33), it follows a good path. Biblical church growth does not accommodate culture but adapts to culture to effectively remove unnecessary barriers to the gospel.

The goal is to glorify God by making disciples who follow Christ, not today's Christian tastes or preferences. Churches that grow will graciously welcome sinful people while showing them there is a better way to live. They understand that any uneasiness should come from a person's realization of sin, not from their way of dress or from their musical taste, political affiliation, or type of car. A faithful church must be relevant to the society it is reaching. They believe what Thomas Jefferson said: "In matters of style, swim with the current. In matters of principle, stand like a rock."[9] Therefore a church must be committed to preaching the message of the Gospel of Jesus Christ using approaches that relate to the culture in which it exists.

Churches that appropriately communicate the unchanging message to a changing culture have a greater chance of seeing biblical church growth occur. While biblical church growth is not primarily concerned with techniques and methodologies, they are vitally important, since communicating the truth of the gospel requires technique. This process can be illustrated as follows. Communicating the unchanging truth of the gospel to people living in a particular cultural context requires a technique or method that is culturally relevant to the people receiving the gospel.

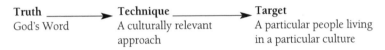

Truth ⟶ **Technique** ⟶ **Target**
God's Word   A culturally relevant   A particular people living
              approach   in a particular culture

While a specific technique may be appropriate for a specific group of people, it is often necessary to adjust one's approach (as Jesus and Paul did) to reach a different people in a different cultural setting.

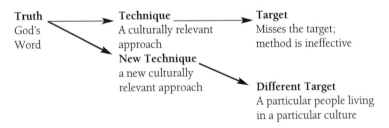

Truth ⟶ **Technique** ⟶ **Target**
God's   A culturally relevant   Misses the target;
Word   approach   method is ineffective
               New Technique
               a new culturally
               relevant approach   **Different Target**
                                        A particular people living
                                        in a particular culture

Life-giving churches understand that we must not sacrifice the gospel on the altar of trends, but we must creatively adapt, integrate, and communicate the Word of God to a changing culture. They understand four critical facts pertaining to the right philosophy. First, *there is no true culture.* God has worked in and through various cultures throughout history and is doing so today. Second, *faithful churches embrace the cultural diversity around them.* While there are aspects of every culture that cannot be embraced, churches must appropriately incarnate themselves in the lives of the people they are seeking to disciple. Third, *faithful churches must study the cultural context around them.* They take on a missiological mind-set by becoming missionaries to the cultures around them. By doing so, they seek to learn as much about the people and cultures as possible, so that they may penetrate every tribe, family, people, or ethnic group with the gospel. Last, *faithful churches select disciple-making methods that are culturally relevant.* They hold on to their biblical values while carefully choosing techniques that are biblically sound and that allow them to faithfully reach the lost.

Our Father God, as we study the growth of Your church, we see before us in our cities and around the world enormous numbers of Your children who are far from home. We see masterless and saviorless men and women, boys and girls, of every region and every tongue, living in their own strength, alienated from You, the constant prey to self and sin. Pour out on Your church we beseech you, O Lord, a great spirit of compassion that she may surge out in effective mission, proclaiming and living the Gospel in such a persuasive and winsome way that the rivers of the water of life may flow through the thirsty land and multitudes perishing in a great famine of the Word of God may drink the water and eat the bread of heaven and live. In Christ's name we pray. Amen.

Donald A. McGavran[10]

Questions to Ask and Answer

1. Does your church tend to approach the popular culture through isolation, domination, or incarnation? Give specific ways it does so.

133

2. Can you identify ways that the popular culture has impacted your church in negative ways? Give some examples.
3. In what ways does your church create unnecessary cultural barriers for the unchurched?
4. Who is most attracted to your church's particular ministry style or cultural texture? Who is not attracted?
5. How easy is it to begin new ministries in your church? When was the last time your church began a culturally relevant ministry for the unchurched in your area?

TEN

The Right Plan
Target Focused

God has willed a ripening harvest field in His world. He also wills that fields white to harvest be found and reaped to the last sheaf.

Donald A. McGavran

A few years ago there was a small church in the Pacific Northwest that had for years neglected any outreach to the community. Notwithstanding, with the arrival of a new pastor, the church leaders decided it was time to begin taking the gospel to the students of a nearby college. The motivation behind their new resolve was the stories the new pastor told of how other churches were seeing students won to Christ through innovative coffeehouse ministries.

Several ideas on how to reach the college students were debated, but the leaders eventually determined that the best approach was to open a coffeehouse near the campus. Most students have time on their hands, especially on Friday evenings, and the leaders were certain a coffeehouse would be well attended by the students, who would be tired of studying all week long. Since other churches were seeing good success using a similar ministry, they felt assured they would also.

Having chosen their method, the church leaders raised the necessary money, renovated a building, contracted with a local band to provide music, recruited the volunteer help, developed advertising, and set a date to open the coffeehouse. Advertising brochures were placed at several locations on campus as well as at local business establishments where students were likely to go. Flyers were distributed in the student union and to students walking on campus.

On opening night, all was in place for the expected crowd. Coffee was prepared, the band was ready to play, and counselors were in attendance. But when the doors were opened, only one person showed up. Since he felt quite awkward being the only person in attendance, he sipped his cup of coffee, listened a short while to the music, and left soon after.

> Despite our timeliness and good intentions, if the method of evangelism we use does not fit the particular harvest, we will be ineffective.
>
> George G. Hunter III[1]

The church leaders decided to double their efforts at advertising and try again. It did no good. After several more weeks of an extremely low turnout, the coffeehouse closed its doors forever. Soon after, the leaders gathered to discuss their unsuccessful project. They had prayed for God's blessing, volunteered their time, advertised well, and even invested their own money. What had gone wrong? Why had God not blessed their efforts? It was only after several months that the answer was discovered. Coffeehouse ministries had indeed proved fruitful in reaching college students, but only near those campuses that had a resident student body. What the church leaders failed to understand was that their college had a commuter student population. The only students who were even around on Friday evenings were those attending classes, which were held during the same time as the coffeehouse hours of operation. In spite of all their hard work, the church had not taken time to study and understand their target audience.

Often well-intentioned churches make mistakes that keep them from experiencing biblical church growth, and one of the major mistakes is to fail to do adequate research to understand the people they

136

The Right Plan—Target Focused

Life-giving churches focus their ministries
on clearly defined groups of responsive people.

are seeking to reach with the gospel. It is important for a church to study the community and culture as well as the Scriptures.

It's good for churches to have a sign that says, "Everyone Welcome." However, without a deliberate strategy in place for reaching the lost, they will experience only accidental church growth. While reaching the whole world with the gospel is the mission of the Christian faith, life-giving churches recognize that the world is made up of many different audiences. Since different groups of people have quite different cultures, needs, and forms of communication, a church that intentionally tries to reach a specific group with the message of Christ will normally be much more effective than one that tries to reach everyone with a general attempt.

Faithful churches follow the eighth principle of biblical church growth—the *right plan:* target focused. Simply stated, *life-giving churches focus their ministries on clearly defined groups of responsive people.*

Reaching the World

At first glance, it may seem that aiming at selected groups of people is not biblical. On further reflection, however, it becomes obvious that it is the only strategic way to actually reach the world for Christ. Think for a moment how God began to redeem the world. From the beginning, God has loved and has been concerned for the entire world, not just certain people. God's desire was (and is) to redeem every tribe, nation, people, and family on the face of the earth. Since God is all-powerful, there must be a way for him to communicate immediately with everyone in the world. Yet how did he go about reaching the world? What plan or strategy did he use? He began by targeting a specific person—Abram (Gen. 12:1–3). His plan started with a clearly defined target audience in the person and family of Abram and worked outwardly from there to the whole world. Abram became a family, then a tribe, and eventually a nation among all the nations of the world. As the family of Abram expanded, its influence impacted more and more people. Of Israel, God said, "I will also make You a light of the nations so that My salvation may reach to the end of the earth" (Isa. 49:6).

The coming of Jesus through the nation of Israel was the key to bringing blessing to all the nations of the world. Indisputably, "God so loved the world, that He gave His only begotten Son, that whoever believes in Him shall not perish, but have eternal life" (John 3:16). Jesus loved the entire world, not just certain select segments of it. He eventually would die for "our sins; and not for ours only, but also for those of the whole world" (1 John 2:2).

To reach the whole world, Jesus began with a defined target audience. His niche was among the Israelites, specifically Galileans. He ate, dressed, spoke, laughed, wept, and lived like a Galilean Israelite. It is no surprise, then, that his tactical plan started with Galileans as his target audience.

It's interesting that Jesus selected for his disciples twelve men who displayed both a heterogeneous and a homogeneous mix. Matthew was an establishment type, Simon the Zealot had a revolutionary background, and Peter, James, and John were all blue-collar workers. Yet they were all Galileans and spoke Aramaic (Matt. 26:73; Mark 14:70; Luke 22:59). No Gentile, Samaritan, Idumean, or even a Hellenistic Jew was part of the Twelve. Jesus gathered an inner circle of men from his target audience. The only exception in the Twelve was Judas Iscariot, who came from Kerioth in the south of Palestine. Eventually, of course, he betrayed the Lord and did not remain a part of the Twelve. His replacement was a Galilean named Matthias (Acts 1:23–26). Similar to the way God chose Abraham and his family, Jesus chose a small group to begin winning the world.

Paul's blueprint for ministry to the world also involved targeting a specific group of people. His heart's desire was always to see the Jews come to faith in Christ (see Rom. 10:1). To him the gospel was for everyone in the world but needed to go to the Jews first, as he declared, "For I am not ashamed of the gospel, for it is the power of God for salvation to everyone who believes, to the Jew first and also to the

Greek" (1:16). Paul's unique calling, however, was to Gentiles. Christ told Ananias concerning Paul, "He is a chosen instrument of Mine, to bear My name before the Gentiles and kings and the sons of Israel" (Acts 9:15). Paul recalled this in his letter to the Galatians. He pointed out to the Galatians that God had set him apart to "preach Him [Christ] among the Gentiles" (Gal. 1:16). The leaders of the Jerusalem church recognized Paul's calling and commissioned both him and Barnabas to go specifically to the Gentiles (2:7–9).

Paul wove his love for the Jews and his calling to the Gentiles into an original strategy. His usual custom was to go first to a synagogue to preach and then move from there to the Gentile God-fearers (Acts 9:20; 13:5; 14:1; see especially 17:1–3). On his first missionary journey, Paul and his companions stopped in Pisidian Antioch and on the Sabbath went to the synagogue (13:13–43). After speaking, Paul and Barnabas were followed by "many of the Jews and of the God-fearing proselytes" (v. 43). The reception from the Jews on the following Sabbath was not so welcoming (vv. 44–45), and Paul affirmed, "We are turning to the Gentiles" (v. 46). To reach the Gentiles, Paul targeted the Jewish synagogue community where he knew there would be God-fearing Gentiles and Gentile proselytes to Judaism. The Jews rejected Paul (except for a few people) in most situations, but he went on to win considerable numbers of the Gentiles and they formed a new church.

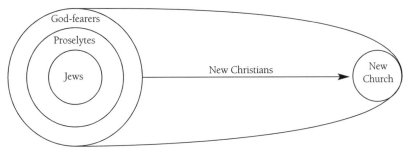

God-fearers
Proselytes
Jews
New Christians
New Church

Synagogue Community

A church should not, of course, be tied so rigidly to a plan or target group that it is insensitive to the leading of the life-giving Spirit in other directions. While it is biblical to focus on a single audience for

> ## F.Y.I.
>
> Churches usually have a limited ministry area. In most situa-
> tions a church will find that 90 percent of its worshipers drive
> less than twenty minutes from their home to church. How
> large is your church's ministry area? How far are people will-
> ing to drive to get to your church? How many minutes does it
> take them to get to church? What implications does this have
> for your ministry?

a short while, the Holy Spirit may direct in supernatural ways to other populations. The early church first took the gospel to the Samaritans due to the persecution that arose in Jerusalem (8:1–5). Philip preached to the Ethiopian eunuch after the Holy Spirit told him to do so. At the same time that Paul was targeting the synagogue community, he remained open to the leading of the life-giving Spirit. In fact Luke records, "They passed through the Phrygian and Galatian region, having been forbidden by the Holy Spirit to speak the word in Asia; and after they came to Mysia, they were trying to go into Bithynia, and the Spirit of Jesus did not permit them" (16:6–7). When a synagogue was not found, Paul and his band sought out the next best place to preach. When they went to Philippi, they found a place of prayer and began preaching Christ to the women assembled there (vv. 11–15).

Having an understanding of one's target audience is a way of deciding what are the most effective methods to win people to Christ while remaining open to supernatural encounters and prayer. A strategic plan is important, but authentic church growth is always supernaturally directed and empowered. As the proverb states, "The mind of man plans his way, but the LORD directs his steps" (Prov. 16:9).

Dining with Jesus

Jesus often created controversy, particularly when he associated with sinners. He made it a practice to eat in the company of acknowledged sinners, a practice that was in direct contrast to that of the Phari-

Touch not the unclean thing

sees. Why did he do something that was so unusual in his day? There seem to be two major reasons. First, table fellowship was a living metaphor for the banquet to come in heaven. Jesus' practice of eating with sinners was an expression of the kingdom in which everyone is invited to God's royal banquet. Jesus was demonstrating that the ones the Pharisees rejected were the very ones God accepted.

Second, Jesus dined with those who were receptive to his message. It was part of his strategy to win the winnable. Dining with receptive people was an important feature of his ministry, as we see in his calling of Matthew the tax collector. After Jesus had called him, Matthew (Levi) gave a reception for Jesus in his home, and "there was a great crowd of tax collectors and other people who were reclining at the table with them" (Luke 5:29). The Pharisees and their scribes noticed this and asked, "Why do you eat and drink with the tax collectors and sinners?" (v. 30). Jesus gave the following answer: "It is not those who are well who need a physician, but those who are sick. I have not come to call the righteous but sinners to repentance" (vv. 31–32). The self-righteous Pharisees, and others like them, were not open to Christ's words; that is, they were not responsive. So Jesus was naturally drawn to those who were receptive to him and his message.

One day as Jesus was walking with his disciples, he saw a great number of people and felt compassion for them "because they were distressed and dispirited like sheep without a shepherd" (Matt. 9:36). Speaking to his disciples, he said, "The harvest is plentiful, but the workers are few. Therefore beseech the Lord of the harvest to send out workers into His harvest" (vv. 37–38). As Jesus looked on the distressed and dispirited people, he understood that some of them were ready to receive his message (they were ripe for harvest). Some people were not going to follow him, but many others were ready to be won, if only workers could be found. Applying this verse to our day and time, we know the following:

1. There are people around us who are ready to receive the gospel.
2. Workers are needed to take the gospel to them.
3. The workers are to focus on those who are receptive, that is, ripe for harvest.

The point of receptivity is illustrated in Matthew 10, immediately following Christ's mention of the harvest being plentiful. Jesus directs the disciples to go only to those who are receptive to the preaching that "the kingdom of heaven is at hand" (10:7). He told them, "As you enter the house, give it your greeting. If the house is worthy, give it your blessing of peace. But if it is not worthy, take back your blessing of peace. Whoever does not receive you, nor heed your words, as you go out of that house or that city, shake the dust off your feet" (vv. 12–14). In other words, the disciples were to spend their time and energy taking the gospel of the kingdom to those who would listen to them—receptive people.

The apostle Paul was selective in his choice of places to preach the gospel. Sometimes the Holy Spirit directed him supernaturally to pass by certain areas. As we have seen, Paul wanted to preach in the Phrygian and Galatian regions and in Mysia and Bithynia, but the Holy Spirit did not permit it (Acts 16:6–8). Instead he led him to Macedonia. At least part of the reason, apparently, was that the people of Macedonia were open to the gospel at that time, as illustrated by the conversions of Lydia (vv. 14–15) and the jailer (vv. 31–40). Later Paul passed through Amphipolis and Apollonia apparently to get to Thessalonica and Berea where the people were more receptive.

The Lord of the harvest has prepared some people to be responsive to the gospel. It is up to us to pray that the Lord will send workers into that harvest field of receptive people and to carefully target our resources and efforts toward them. Thus biblical church growth seeks to identify the most responsive people and groups in a church's ministry area. These are called "right end peoples." A church can, through research, determine the relative receptivity and resistance to the gospel of people in its community and plot them on a continuum (see diagram next page). For example, defined people groups in a community could be labeled A, B, C, and so forth. After studying this mosaic of people, they could be plotted on a continuum to demonstrate where they fall at the present time regarding their receptivity to the gospel. In the diagram it is easy to see that groups A and W have been determined to be receptive (right end peoples), while groups K and Y are viewed as not receptive (left end peoples). The groups in

142

the middle are perhaps receptive, and it will take time to determine which direction they are heading.

Determining where people are in their receptivity or resistance to the gospel is especially important when deciding what methodology to use for evangelism. When people are very receptive to the gospel (right end peoples), they will respond to many different approaches. At the other extreme, when people are very resistant (left end peoples), they reject just about any approach. The people in the middle will respond only to particular methods that the church might use. And as you might have guessed, most people are somewhere in the middle, which makes selecting a proper method crucial to biblical church growth. In general, we find right end peoples in areas where churches are growing through conversions to Christ, where changes are taking place, where large masses of people reside close together, and where people are moving in rather than out of the community. Churches that desire to experience biblical church growth seek to identify right end peoples and also the methods that will work with the people in the middle of the continuum.

God honors many methods, but the methods we use will determine whom we reach for Christ. People who were brought to Christ through an event, such as vacation Bible school, Sunday school, or a revival, tend to think that invitations to events are the best method for evangelism. An invitation approach will work for a target audience that is comfortable with attending church events, but such a method will prove ineffective with a target group that feels uncomfortable at church events. Selecting the right method is being "response-able," that is, having the ability to do *what* needs to be done *when* it needs to be done. One writer contends: "In a growing church, the method is never to be considered as important as the task. Under God, a healthy church possesses a growth conscience which prompts it to 'outreach at any cost' and then finds the methods which will prove successful."[2] This is where needs fit in. As George Hunter suggests, "Churches grow as they identify people with needs that the church can minister to, either by extending ministries already in place or building new ministries."[3] Needy people tend to be responsive people.

Studying the Community

The mission of the church is to the entire world. As such, the gospel is inclusive and broad in its target, and it is at the universal church level that such inclusiveness is most obvious. At the local church level, however, growing congregations realize that while wanting to be accessible to all people, they are most faithful and fruitful when they have a defined target audience. Targeting specific people groups living in a specific culture is not unloving to the rest of the community; it is just facing the fact that a church has to begin reaching the whole world somewhere specific.

Churches that desire to experience biblical church growth need to look carefully at themselves as a church and then at the community they would like to reach. Essentially they ask and answer the following five questions:

- Where are we?
- Where should we be headed?
- What steps will take us there?
- How can we align our resources to support our vision?
- How are we doing?

The First Question

In asking the question, "Where are we?" a church attempts to determine its current situation. For biblical church growth it is vital to have accurate information rather than simple guesswork. For example, quite often churches feel they are doing well in evangelism, but then research reveals they are doing poorly. An in-depth study of what is

144

Smart Move

Appoint a task force of seven people to study the demographic makeup of your church. Ask them to find out what
group or groups of people your church primarily attracts and
which group or groups your church has difficulty reaching.
What insights and recommendations can they suggest so that
your church could be more effective in its outreach?

---

actually happening in the life of a church is the best way to determine
its current health.

The Second Question

"Where should we be headed?" implies that solid demographic
and psychographic analysis of the community will be used to help a
church determine proper target groups and methods for reaching
them. Demographic information points out the hard facts about people in a church's ministry area, such as how many people live in the
community and their marital, educational, and socioeconomic sta-
tus. Psychographic information points out the soft data of the community, such as how people think and their personal preferences and
tastes.

Occasionally churches grow without consciously targeting responsive people. Study of such situations usually reveals that a church is
targeting a receptive audience, if only by accident, or more correctly
by God's sovereign design. The fact of the matter is that every congregation has its own unique texture, and it attracts and keeps certain kinds of people. It also repels and rejects certain kinds of people, although not on purpose. While a responsive target audience
can be discovered accidentally, it is much better to define a receptive
target audience and then to select an effective strategy and plan. A
target audience must be defined spiritually, culturally, and geographically. This is where demographics and psychographics come
into play.

145

For biblical church growth, demographic and psychographic information must never be allowed to dictate our values and mission. Wise leaders use such information, however, to understand their community and inform their strategies. Lyle Schaller says, "The more precisely your audience is defined, the easier it will be to reach, serve, and challenge your constituency."[4] As a church studies its community, it will be able to assess the receptivity and resistance of various target groups, which will help it identify right end peoples. The following two stories illustrate how this can be done effectively.

> We are in no position to know the target population's culture, values, and life-style, or their felt needs, driving motivation, and points of contact with Christians, or their images, hang-ups, barriers, and doubts regarding Christianity, or the language they understand and the response patterns that are natural to them, or where and when they may assemble to consider the gospel— unless we ask them.
>
> George G. Hunter III[5]

One church I worked with a number of years ago wanted to reach out with the gospel to people in their city. Like most churches, they had a limited amount of time and money to invest. In an effort to be faithful with their resources, the church leaders decided to study three communities in their city to see which area would be the most responsive. The church surveyed the three areas and issued invitations to attend church. Then over the next few weeks, they kept careful records to see if anyone from these communities did in fact visit. After a few weeks, it became obvious that one of the areas seemed very responsive. Several people from that particular part of the city did visit the church, giving at least a preliminary indication that the people in that part of the city were receptive to the gospel.

A good friend of mine who pastors a midsized church wanted to identify the best way to follow up on people who attended his church. In an effort to discover the best approach, he devised three different strategic plans for following up on visitors. For four months he used one approach, then switched to the second method for another four months, and finally the third strategy was used for the final four months of the year. By keeping careful records, he was able to see clearly which follow-up strategy worked best. The following year, he began using the most successful approach.

The Final Questions

The third question, "What steps will take us there?" encourages the church to develop a plan to address the needs of people. This is when plans are made to implement proper methods and equip members to use their spiritual gifts. It is at this juncture that churches desiring biblical church growth make certain that every ministry of the church follows its mission and vision.

"How can we align our resources to support our vision?" is the fourth major question. By asking this, a church is seeking to resolve financial and personnel issues. Unless a church puts money and people behind its plans, nothing tends to change.

Finally, a church asks, "How are we doing?" Serious and honest evaluations are done once or twice a year to see if the church's plans are indeed being followed. Where needed, critical corrections are made along the way to ensure the fulfillment of the church's vision.

Growth Creates Growth

Once a church begins to grow, it will find that subsequent growth comes more easily, because the size of a church has a major effect on how many groups can be effectively targeted. In general, the smaller a church is, the more important it is to have a narrowly defined target group. When a church is small, it does not have the resources to reach a broad audience. For example, if a church of fifty people is in a community of 100,000, how will it effectively reach the community for Christ? Logically, the church must start somewhere. If its leadership carefully studies the community, they will find a field "white for harvest" that God has made ready for it to reach. As they study the target audience and select a culturally relevant method to reach them, the church will be fruitful.

Most often the target audience is one that is a near neighbor, that is, a group of people culturally similar to the church. As an example, suppose a church is designated E on a continuum (see diagram). If it is a small church, it will usually be most effective in reaching people in groups D and F who are their near neighbors. It may have some people attend who come from the remaining groups, but not very many.

Smaller Church

On the other hand, if the church is larger, it will usually be able to reach several different groups. A larger church is actually a congregation of congregations, so the larger a church is, the greater the mosaic of people, the greater the variety of ministries, the greater the resources, and thus the greater number of target audiences it can effectively reach with the gospel.

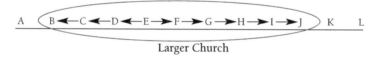

Larger Church

When you think about it, it is possible for the church universal to reach everyone, but impossible for a local church to reach everyone. That is why there can be no one model for ministry and no one method for evangelism. It takes a multitude of models and methods because there are multitudes of different people who need to be reached.

In the same way that missionaries immerse themselves in the culture and among the people they are trying to reach, a local church must study the culture and people it is seeking to reach. If a church is going to accomplish its mission, it cannot afford to clothe its message in words, music, and styles that will not be understood by its target audience. Churches cannot continue to use seventeenth-century language, eighteenth-century architecture, and twentieth-century methods if they are going to win the twenty-first-century world to Christ. If they do, the people they are called to reach will ignore the message. At the same time, the unbelieving world cannot be allowed to prescribe the content of the church's message. A church should not be shaped by the values of the marketplace. This is part of the balance of being *in the world* but not *of the world*.

Lord, grant us discrimination, the power of careful, correct thinking, as we seek to propagate the gospel and multiply churches and treat men and women as our kith and kin and respect them while evangelizing them. Grant us your Spirit. Teach us particularly how to deal with the customs and ways that are precious to others, so that the gospel may be heard and obeyed. This we ask in Jesus' name. Amen.

Donald A. McGavran[6]

Questions to Ask and Answer

1. How many different groups of people can you identify within a twenty-minute drive of your church?
2. Based on the answer to question one, what group or groups does your church tend to attract and/or reach? Which groups do you find difficult to attract and/or reach? Why?
3. Describe the main group or groups of people your church reaches. Where do they live? What do they do for recreation? What do they like or dislike about church? What is their attitude toward Jesus Christ and the gospel? What would be the best way to communicate to them?
4. In what ways has your church developed special outreach ministries specifically targeted to the various groups of people in

your ministry area? What new ministries are needed within the next two years?

5. Which groups of people appear to be most responsive to the gospel at this time? Which ones seem to be the least responsive? Are there groups of people your church should be reaching but are not?

ELEVEN

The Right Procedure

Simple Structure

Many leaders, both laymen and ministers, get tied to programs which have little to do with the propagation of the Gospel and nothing to do with finding the lost. A minister can be trapped in "splendid work whether the church grows or not."

Donald A. McGavran

The church was almost paralyzed. After nearly a half century of faithful ministry that had resulted in a weekly attendance of nearly 2,200 members, the church could no longer function. A total of sixty-plus committees (the exact number was unknown) were bumping into one another. No one seemed to know which committee was responsible for what particular ministry. Each committee overlapped another one to the point that nothing could be decided without stepping on the proverbial toes of some other committee. The result was a church that ministered week to week without any clear direction.

Though, to the casual observer, Sunday ministries came off looking good, in reality the church was going nowhere. Bureaucracy was choking the life out of its programs. New ministries could not get approved, and visionary leaders left the church in frustration. An average of 70 new members were welcomed into the church each quarter. Unknown to most, however, was the fact that an average of 125 people were leaving the church every three months, for a net loss of 55 people each quarter. This slow leak had been going on for a number of years, but due to the large size of the church, the losses were unnoticed by most members.

As leaders began to admit that the problems were overwhelming and that something had to be done, answers began to be formulated. The old system had operated well for nearly fifty years but was now so inept that it demanded more than it was providing. Committees spent most of their time seeking to justify their existence rather than providing service or effective ministry to the church. Members of the nominating committee struggled each year to find enough volunteers to fill the numerous vacancies created by departing committee members. Something had to be done.

Church leaders designed a new system that would allow the church to reorganize itself to overcome bureaucracy without slipping into the opposite problem of dictatorship. The congregation streamlined its structure by putting its affairs into the hands of the paid staff, one main board of elders, and three committees. Moving from sixty-plus committees to only three was the key. It released nearly six hundred people for service in more fruitful areas of ministry. Surprisingly, the congregation agreed to the change, most likely because they understood that the system was squeezing the life out of the church's ministry.

At its core, the church is a living organism, and Jesus Christ is its head (Eph. 5:23; Col. 1:18). All organisms exhibit organizational systems that allow them to function in a healthy manner. The human body demonstrates this truth. Within the human body are numerous life systems that allow the living organism to function well. The neurological, cardiovascular, muscular, digestive, and arterial systems interlink to maintain a healthy body. In a similar manner the overall systems in a local church must function well together for biblical church growth to occur. If the church system gets clogged, like arteries sometimes do in a human body, a church ceases to function well and biblical growth is not as likely to happen. That is why churches that desire biblical church growth follow the *right procedure:* simple

> ## The Right Procedure—Simple Structure
>
> Life-giving churches employ simple organizational systems.

structure. Simply stated, *life-giving churches employ simple organizational systems.*

The Spirit's Instructions

When one looks to the Bible to discover what instructions the life-giving Spirit gives regarding church organization, it is surprising to find very few specifics. No direct decreed statements are given on what the structure of a church should be. The Holy Spirit does, of course, enlighten the church on the qualifications for the offices of elder and deacon (1 Tim. 3:1–13; Titus 1:5–9; and 1 Tim. 3:11 may be giving the qualifications for the office of deaconess). Other than these specific instructions, there is no direction in the New Testament for a complete church structure or system.

Some help is found in the descriptions of the early church's practices and procedures. At least four principles for church structure are evident in narrative passages. First, *it is evident that as a church grows, certain persons need to be placed in charge of specific ministries.* This we see in Acts 6. The church had grown and the ministry to widows was getting out of control. The solution to this difficulty was to place certain people over this ministry to manage it.

Second, *every believer is responsible for and capable of relating directly to God* (Rom. 5:1–5; 1 Tim. 2:5; Heb. 4:14–16). Church structure is not meant to provide any redemptive access to the Lord. There is only "one God, and one mediator also between God and men, the man Christ Jesus" (1 Tim. 2:5). Believers are capable of worshiping, learning, discerning, and serving as the life-giving Spirit personally leads them.

Third, *each believer is gifted to serve the entire body* (Romans 12; 1 Corinthians 12; 1 Peter 4). Among other things, this means that each person is important to the church. It is implied, because each person is a believer priest and gifted to serve, that it is necessary for everyone to have some input into the fellowship of the community. The apostles observed the seriousness of this by asking the church members to select their own ministry leaders (Acts 6:1–7).

Fourth, *order is vital to the continued health of a church.* Speaking about the misuse of spiritual gifts, Paul reminds the Corinthians: "All things must be done properly and in an orderly manner" (1 Cor. 14:40). By application, order extends to every area of a church's life, function, and structure. It is not likely that God will bless a mess.

Beyond these principles, the early church appears to have adopted a form of church structure that they were most familiar with and that fit the culture in which they lived. For example, the first church followed the pattern of the Jewish synagogue and selected elders to serve as the rulers. As the church moved throughout history, it seems that the life-giving Spirit allowed each church to develop a unique structure suitable to the culture in which it existed. It should therefore be no surprise that in the days of monarchies the Episcopal system of church structure developed. It was the system the people were most comfortable with, and the church adopted it in the same way the early disciples adopted the synagogue model. As people became more educated and involved in the political process in various countries, the Presbyterian form of church government evolved, offering a representative format. When governments became democratic, churches reasonably started using congregational forms.

The Bible and church history point to two main conclusions regarding church structure. First, *the life-giving Spirit is more concerned about function than form.* Throughout the Bible, many didactic instructions are given regarding the various functions of a church. A church is to study God's Word, fellowship together, practice continual prayer, serve and forgive one another, and in short "do all in the name of the Lord Jesus" (see Col. 3:12–17; Acts 2:42–47). Presumably Scripture allows any form of church structure, as long as it encourages the proper functions that characterize a biblical church. Some church structures appear to encourage biblical functions more than others, but flexibility seems to be the norm rather than rigidity in this regard.

154

The second conclusion we can draw from the Bible and from church history is that *the life-giving Spirit is earnestly concerned with reaching every tribe, nation, people, and family.* In order to do so, local churches must exist in each *ethne* of the whole world. If only one form of church structure had been dictated, it would have been impossible for all the *ethnes* of the world to be reached. One construct of church form could not have adapted to all the cultures and subcultures found in the world. However, by leaving the form of church structure open, the Holy Spirit made certain that the church could exist in every culture on the face of the earth. By being flexible in form, a church can adapt to any culture and keep its focus on the functions that are characteristic of a church.

Churches that desire to experience biblical church growth realize that God has given limited instructions on what the structure of a local church should be. The life-giving Spirit's silence respecting specific organizational structure for a church is intended to allow each church to adapt appropriately to the culture in which it ministers. Whatever structure is selected, it should do two things: maximize ministry and minimize maintenance. In general, complex bureaucratic forms of church structure restrict growth, while simple free-flowing forms release growth.

Life Cycle Insights

Organizational structures do not cause growth, but they do control the rate and size of growth. They can stop growth from taking place or provide channels for additional growth. This can be understood by looking at the typical life cycle of a church.

Every organization is different, but there are generalizations that help us understand how organizational structure contributes to a church's growth and decline. When growth is charted, many churches show typical patterns of growth, plateau, and decline. Churches follow essentially the same life cycle pattern as do humans. The human life cycle begins with birth, moves on to childhood, progresses through adolescence, adulthood, and eventually to old age and death.

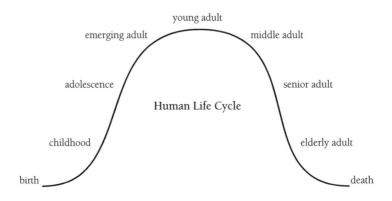

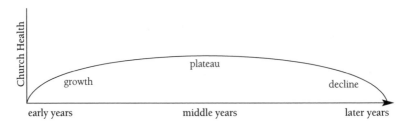

Life cycles are recognized as a natural part of life. Ecclesiastes records: "There is an appointed time for everything. And there is a time for every event under heaven—a time to give birth and a time to die; a time to plant and a time to uproot what is planted" (Eccles. 3:1–2). The apostle John reveals in Revelation 2–3 that the earliest churches experienced the normal process of life cycle events. St. John's Syndrome, as this life cycle process is often called, refers to the natural aging process churches go through. The typical church life cycle appears as follows.

The first fifteen to twenty years of a church's life cycle are typically its most dynamic ones. During this time vision and understanding of the church's purpose are extremely clear. Morale is high, and this helps to draw people into participation and sacrificial giving. There is a feeling of mutual dependency, and all members are willing to serve. Attitudes are positive, and people are open to new ways of doing ministry. Changes are easily adopted and integrated into the church structure. Because of minimal organization, there is spontaneity and flexibility in decision making. Structures are created in response to the needs, with the function of ministry determining the form. These attitudes and structure allow for a period of rapid growth of the ministry.

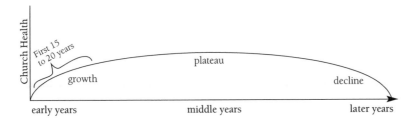

Momentum gained from the first years of rapid growth continues to propel the church forward in effective ministry for another twenty years. During this phase of a church's life cycle, morale reaches an all-time high as the majority of the congregation accepts the vision and mission of the church. New members are quickly involved in ministry at a high level of enthusiasm. With the increasing number of people and programs, there is a need for the church to establish rules to regulate and control the expanding ministry. Generally, however, new ministries continue to be started based on the needs of people and the vision of ministry to the community.

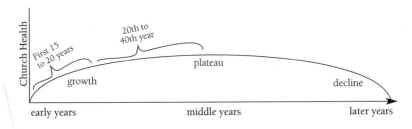

Without realizing what is taking place, a church gradually begins to find itself on a ministry plateau. After forty years of effective ministry, the church discovers that the original vision and mission that propelled the church forward have been forgotten. Current members have a poor understanding of the purpose of the church, and this results in ministry being done "because we've always done it that way." Some people begin to assume others will do the work, and original members pull back from service saying, "We've done our part." Morale declines as people find it harder to establish new programs to serve the real needs of those inside and outside the church. The plateauing of a church almost always involves increased bureaucracy, emphasis on maintenance, and unwillingness to change. Now the forms of ministry determine the function as organizational structures create needs rather than respond to needs.

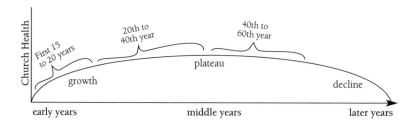

If nothing is done to change the trend, a church eventually disintegrates into a period of stagnation and decline over the next twenty or more years. Eventually the church's sense of mission is lost, resulting in little concern for fulfilling the Great Commission. Programs are eliminated due to a lack of leadership and participation. Volunteers are difficult to find and members say, "It's the staff's job. That's what we pay them to do." Morale drops to an all-time low as leaders and members experience frustration and despair. People blame others for the decline in church attendance and rationalize an unwillingness to change by saying, "We've never done it that way before." Rigid structures prevent new ministries from being started and drive visionary leaders away to other churches where new ideas are accepted and implemented.

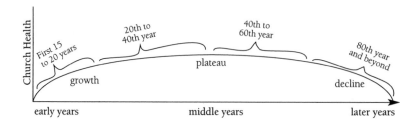

Smart Move

Draw your own picture of the life cycle of a church and then place an X on the curve where you believe your church is currently. Briefly explain why you placed the X at that spot. Then, based on the brief descriptions of each stage of a church's life cycle noted above, describe your present church structure. Would you say your church's structure is "maximizing ministry and minimizing maintenance" or "maximizing maintenance and minimizing ministry"? What needs to be done to simplify your church's structure?

The structural flexibility of a church in its beginning years provides for a maximizing of ministry and a minimizing of maintenance. At the end of a church's life cycle, the situation is reversed and a church maximizes maintenance and minimizes ministry. In its first years the biblical functions create the forms of ministry, but in later years the forms strangle the functions.

From the life cycle perspective of organization, the benefits of a simple structure are many. Simple structure keeps the focus on the vision and mission of the church. Few committees and boards allow for a clear and accessible decision-making climate. Simple structure emphasizes relationships rather than organization. People are seen as more important than programs. Participation by gifted people is encouraged. Creativity is praised, and this attracts visionary people who are committed to doing whatever it takes to respond to Christ's command to make disciples. The organism tends to be more stable, and less maintenance is required.

A church with a bureaucratic structure becomes a maze of maintenance. Multiple committees lose their sense of purpose and direction but continue to fight for their preservation. Money, facilities, and energy are expended on just keeping the church solvent, and no one asks where the church is heading. Abundant energy is used up just keeping the system intact without asking how effectively the system is serving people.

Simplifying Structure

Since its beginning, the church has had characteristics of organization. The early Christians selected church leaders (Acts 6:1–7), they had specific times of meeting (John 20:19, 26; Acts 20:7; 1 Cor. 16:2), church discipline was exercised (Rom. 16:17; 1 Cor. 5:13; 14:34), and money was raised (1 Cor. 16:1–2; 2 Cor. 8:1–5). However, as noted previously, no prescribed form of church government or organization was dictated. Believers were (and are) free to choose the organizational structure that best suited their circumstances and maximized the biblical functions of the church, such as prayer, gifted ministry, and caregiving.

A simple outline of structure is evident in the Bible, however, that should be reflected to some degree in all churches. First, *the congregation is to choose its leaders.* From the beginning of the church, the primary responsibility of the people, from an organizational sense, has been to choose their leaders. Before the church was officially formed, those who were to initiate its beginning met to select a replacement for Judas. "So they put forward two men, Joseph called Barsabbas (who was also called Justus), and Matthias. . . . And they drew lots for them, and the lot fell to Matthias; and he was added to the eleven apostles" (Acts 1:23, 26). When problems arose in the distribution of food to widows, the people "chose Stephen, a man full of faith and of the Holy Spirit, and Philip, Prochorus, Nicanor, Timon, Parmenas and Nicolas, a proselyte from Antioch" (6:5). In cooperation with the Holy Spirit, they selected and sent out the first missionaries (13:1–3). During times of conflict, the members of the church appointed leaders to deal with controversial and doctrinal issues (15:2).

Specific guidelines are given for choosing leaders, with the emphasis always given to the godly character of those being selected. The believers were to select men of "good reputation, full of the Spirit and of wisdom" (6:3). Leaders were to be "above reproach, the husband of one wife, temperate, prudent, respectable, hospitable, able to teach, not addicted to wine or pugnacious, but gentle, peaceable, free from the love of money" (1 Tim. 3:2–3; see also vv. 4–13 and Titus 1:5–16). In other words, the organizational duty of church members is to select godly leaders.

The second structural requisite is that *the chosen leaders are to lead*. As we saw in chapter 7, the three designations of pastor, elder, and bishop denote one leadership office (Titus 1:5–9; 1 Peter 5:1–2). Leaders are to "be on guard for yourselves and for all the flock, among which the Holy Spirit has made you overseers, to shepherd the church of God which He purchased with His own blood" (Acts 20:28). The apostle Peter exhorts the leaders of the church: "Shepherd the flock of God among you, exercising oversight not under compulsion, but voluntarily, according to the will of God" (1 Peter 5:2). Leaders are to exercise oversight *(episkopeo)*, meaning they are "to look upon or over" the people God has placed in their care. Such leadership of the flock includes pastoral care but also protection and guidance. The members of the congregation are not to lead the flock. This directive is given: "Obey your leaders and submit to them, for they keep watch over your souls as those who will give an account. Let them do this with joy and not with grief, for this would be unprofitable for you" (Heb. 13:17). In other words, the organizational duty of church leaders is to feed, protect, and lead the flock of God that is under their care. The organizational duties of the members are to carefully choose godly leaders and then let them lead. Leaders must wisely involve the congregation in ministry decisions, but the role of leadership is particular to them, while the role of serving with one's spiritual gifts is particular to the congregation (Eph. 4:11–12).

In practice, the operational structure of a church would appear in the general form that follows: The congregation chooses godly leaders whom they can trust with the affairs of the congregation. Then the chosen leaders determine a form of organization that will maximize ministry and minimize maintenance. In small churches in which members can be knowledgeable about the church's total ministry, it would be logical at times for the entire congregation to be involved in making decisions. In larger churches in which many members may have extremely limited understanding of the church ministry, it is reasonable for the chosen leaders to make nearly all of the decisions. In a situation in which church members are immature believers, it would be acceptable for the leaders to be directive. In overseeing a congregation that is spiritually mature, it would be sensible for the leaders to operate by consensus. In each of these and other potential situations, the form of church structure is biblical, as the leaders are free

The Bottom Line

Churches grow as they develop an organizational structure that allows them to take advantage of ministry opportunities.

Gary Martin and Gary McIntosh[1]

to select the operational format that will provide maximum ministry and minimum maintenance.

Leaders who operate in a simple structure encourage new ministries rather than discourage them. The dividends for leaders are several. First, leaders no longer need to bear the burden of initiating and carrying out new ministries, because they are born at the grassroots level. Second, leaders no longer need to be threatened by new innovative ideas, because they expect members to initiate such ministries. Third, since everyone is on the same team rooting for the same cause, adversarial relationships are minimized. Most of all, a simple structure equips the "saints for the work of service, to the building up of the body of Christ" (Eph. 4:12).

Organizations are undergoing significant restructuring due to the rapid pace of change in our world. "Some of the new organizing principles are worship and music styles (from traditional to contemporary), disciple making style (from curriculum-based to a spiritual journey), polity and governance (from congregational or board to staff and elder), and change strategies (from allocation to innovation)."[2] Each of these approaches to organization is biblical, and each congregation is free under the guidance of the life-giving Spirit to select the approach that best fits its situation. However, the more streamlined the overall structure is, the more potential the church will have for biblical church growth.

We gather before You, O Lord our God, as those whom You have called . . . called to be Your ministers and missionaries and adminis-

trators. Into our hands, good Lord, You have delivered considerable ability and resources. You have appointed us as stewards, and You have given us responsibilities, and from us You will require an accounting. And we are told that it is required of a steward that he be found faithful. We discharge our duties, O Lord, in a very complex world where many priorities war within us and without us. We live in such a welter of demands. So many people are shouting that we should follow what they think is important, and our own hearts, Lord, are pulled this way and that. So we cry to You, our compassionate God; send out Your light and Your truth. Let them lead us. Help us discern what is Your clear command and where we are left to do what we think best. Help us weigh most carefully between appealing courses of action. Show the clear light of Your revelation on our pathway. And above all, O God, give us the courage to walk the paths which You show to us. In Christ's name. Amen.

Donald A. McGavran[3]

Questions to Ask and Answer

1. What organizational structure does your church ascribe to? What are the strengths or weaknesses of your structure?
2. How does your church structure encourage church growth? How does it create barriers to church growth?
3. Based on the general life cycle of a church described in this chapter, where would you place your church? Why do you put it there? What implications does this have for your church?
4. If you could simplify your church's organizational structure, what would you do?
5. Does your church's structure minimize maintenance and maximize ministry or maximize maintenance and minimize ministry? Describe specific ways this happens.

TWELVE

Mix It Right

If a church is not growing, keep adjusting the ingredients—more of this, less of that. When the church starts growing, you have the right mix.

Donald McGavran and Win Arn

Like many grandmothers, mine was an outstanding cook. Her specialty was baking pies, cakes, and dinner rolls. Just before she retired, she would rise between 3:00 and 4:00 A.M. in the morning to go to her job at a local grocery store. In those days some grocery stores had lunch counters that served breakfast, lunch, and dinner. Grandma's job was to bake the pies to be sold in the store and at the food counter. She often mixed and baked more than one hundred pies in a single day, and she made them all without ever using a recipe.

Many times customers who ate at the lunch counter would ask for her recipes. When she had time, she would gladly scratch out a recipe on whatever piece of paper she could find. Delighted customers drove home with her freshly scribbled recipe, hoping they could create a pie or cake or dinner roll that tasted as good as hers. Unfortunately, as you might guess, their baked goods never came out of the oven looking or tasting as good as hers.

The reason was the recipe. Grandma just knew how to select and mix the ingredients correctly. After cooking for nearly fifty-five years, it just came naturally to her. Cooking was second nature to her, but rarely could she write out a recipe correctly. Without the right recipe and proper mixing of the eggs, flour, sugar, spices, and extracts, it is next to impossible to have a delicious-tasting result.

In a similar fashion, biblical church growth occurs when the right ingredients are properly blended to create dynamic synergy. The necessary ingredients are, of course, the nine principles described throughout this book. However, it is as they interact together that dynamic growth takes place.

Dynamic Growth

The early church experienced dynamic growth. This is evident even after a casual reading of the historical account of the church's beginnings in the Book of Acts. When the first disciples returned to Jerusalem, "about one hundred and twenty persons were together" (Acts 1:15). After Peter's sermon on the Day of Pentecost, "there were added about three thousand souls" (2:41), and the growth kept going as the Lord added "to their number day by day those who were being saved" (v. 47). A short while later Peter and John were arrested for healing a lame man. Peter preached a second sermon, and "many of those who had heard the message believed; and the number of the men came to be about five thousand" (4:4). Soon the church's growth was so dynamic that Luke quit counting and declared, "All the more believers in the Lord, multitudes of men and women, were constantly added to their number" (5:14). When godly leadership resulted in the delegation of work to qualified servants, "the word of God kept on spreading; and the number of the disciples continued to increase greatly in Jerusalem, and a great many of the priests were becoming obedient to the faith" (6:7). Shortly after Paul's conversion, "the church throughout all Judea and Galilee and Samaria enjoyed peace, being built up; and going on in the fear of the Lord and in the comfort of the Holy Spirit, it continued to increase" (9:31). In the wake of the persecution in Jerusalem, the scattered Christians journeyed to Antioch, where "the hand of the Lord was with them, and a large number who believed turned to the Lord" (11:21). Eventually the total number of Christians became so large that Luke stopped counting people and started counting churches, since they "were increasing in number daily" (16:5).

Luke's description of the numerical growth of the church is scattered throughout Acts. Following the pattern of Acts 1:8, he traces this growth, beginning in Jerusalem (2:47; 4:4; 6:1, 7), through Judea and Samaria (9:31; 12:24), and into the uttermost parts of the earth (16:5; 19:20). The emphasis on numerical growth is difficult to ignore.

Luke's fondness for numbers is not accidental; rather it is a key aspect of his purpose in writing Acts. He is not just giving a description of what happened historically but attempting to demonstrate that numerical growth is to be a natural expectation of a healthy church. Numerical growth is to be expected as part of God's blessing.

He uses two primary words to describe the growth of the church: *grow (auxano)* and *multiply (plethyno)*. The first word, *to grow*, is used in agriculture. The second word, *to multiply*, is often used in the context of counting people or things. These two words are used together in Acts 6:7 and 12:24. In both places the emphasis is purely on numerical growth. Luke's use of these two words together is theologically significant in several ways. First, *it calls to mind a similar combination of words from Genesis*. Five times God uses the phrase "be fruitful and multiply," twice in reference to nature and three times in reference to humanity (Gen. 1:22, 28; 8:17; 9:1, 7).[1] "Both in the context of creation and in the aftermath of the Noahic flood, God's mandate is to populate the earth—to increase in number."[2]

Second, *the same phrase is used to describe the numerical growth of Israel*. Isaac blessed his son Jacob and sent him away saying, "May God Almighty bless you and *make you fruitful and multiply you*, that you may become a company of peoples" (Gen. 28:3, italics mine; see also 35:11; 47:27; 48:4; Lev. 26:9). The combination of the words *fruitful* and *multiply* clearly refers to the blessing of God in numerical increase, for "the sons of Israel were fruitful and increased greatly, and multiplied, and became exceedingly mighty, so that the land was filled with them" (Exod. 1:7).

Third, *the combination of these two words is used in conjunction with the promise of the coming Messiah.* With words that sound strikingly familiar to the Great Commission, Jeremiah prophesies, "Then I Myself will gather the remnant of My flock out of all the countries where I have driven them and bring them back to their pasture, and they will be fruitful and multiply" (Jer. 23:3). While there is still a coming future fulfillment of this prophecy specifically for Israel, the prophecy has been fulfilled, at least in part, in the church. As the church takes the gospel to all the tribes, people, families, and clans of the earth, the church is fulfilling its mandate to be fruitful and multiply—increasing in number.

Twice Luke refers to the increasing of the word of the Lord as a metaphor for the numerical growth of the church. He reports, "The word of God kept on spreading" (Acts 6:7), and "The word of the Lord continued to grow and to be multiplied" (12:24). Paul uses a similar statement when he tells the Thessalonians: "Brethren, pray for us that the word of the Lord will spread rapidly and be glorified, just as it did also with you" (2 Thess. 3:1). Paul expects the word of God to result in numerical growth, even as it did with the Thessalonians. He noted this fact in his first letter to the Thessalonians, when he wrote: "For the word of the Lord has sounded forth from you, not only in Macedonia and Achaia, but also in every place your faith toward God has gone forth, so that we have no need to say anything. For they themselves report about us what kind of a reception we had with you, and how you turned to God from idols to serve a living and true God" (1 Thess. 1:8–9). Paul expects churches to grow numerically as believers conduct themselves "with wisdom toward outsiders, making the most of the opportunity" (Col. 4:5). He counts on the Colossians to pray that "God will open up to us a door for the word" (v. 3), which is an obvious reference to a desire for numerical church growth (see Acts 14:27).

While it is true that the writers of the Epistles focus more on spiritual growth than numerical growth, this is most likely due to their assumption that people already expected numerical growth. No doubt the writers of the Epistles thought the numerical growth all around them made that goal obvious. Since they did not need to demonstrate

> ## The Bottom Line
>
> Does the King of Kings still care about the lost? He does! And churches that wish to experience growth must care also. The aim of biblical church growth is numerical increase of the church. It is not, however, numbers for the sake of numbers but numbers for the sake of people. We must always remember that no numbers means no people.

that numerical growth was to be expected, they turned their focus on the internal workings of the church.

Against this background it seems apparent that Luke's accounting of church growth is more than a passing interest. It is Luke's purpose to demonstrate that the growth of the church is a natural part of God's blessing. He blessed Israel with numerical growth, and he will bless the church with the same. It is part of the nature of the life-giving God to bless his people with fruitful ministry as they obediently follow his command to disciple the nations. The fact that numerous churches are not growing does not negate the truth that God desires to bless them with numerical growth. It does indicate that, for many complex reasons, a significant number of churches are not cooperating with God for biblical church growth.

When Jesus first used the word *church* (Matt. 16:18), he implied that both the universal church and local churches would grow. The universal church is a concrete entity. It is made up of countable disciples and grows in identifiable locations among real people. The universal church grows as local churches win new converts and assimilate them into the body, thus increasing their membership. The universal church grows as new churches are planted in every tribe, family, people, and clan of the world. At its heart, biblical church growth is more about church planting than just seeing a single church grow. The Great Commission demands church planting, as it is the only logical way to reach all the nations. The apostle Paul, and others, demonstrated the effectiveness of church planting in making disciples, and the churches were "increasing in number daily" due to his efforts (Acts 16:5).

Numerical growth is to be expected in local churches. Some local churches grow dramatically, others more slowly, and, of course, some do not grow at all. However, if the universal church is to grow, as Christ promised it would, local congregations must win people to Christ and assimilate new disciples into the body.

Multiplication Effect

Numerical growth is a biblical expectation for churches. Yet it is obvious that some churches do not grow, while others explode with dynamic growth. Why is this? Part of the answer is found in understanding the effect created by the interaction of the core principles of biblical church growth.

The potential for local churches to experience biblical church growth is directly related to the dynamic interaction or mix of the nine biblical principles already discussed: the right premise, the right priority, the right process, the right power, the right pastor, the right people, the right philosophy, the right plan, and the right procedure. The more principles a church is effectively using, the greater the potential for growth. The fewer principles activated in a church, the lower the potential for growth.

One way to understand the variations of growth potential is by observing the effect of multiplication. As a church builds on each principle, there is an empowering that takes place as each principle interacts with each of the others. As an illustration, assume that we give each principle a numerical value of 2. We might assume a church's growth potential would rise gradually as it faithfully employs each of the nine principles (see first column below). In reality, however, the effect of employing each growth principle is multiplication

> The church as it grows anywhere always grows in specific congregations; it never grows in general. Growth occurs as specific congregations increase their memberships (expansion) and as churches plant new congregations (extension).
>
> Donald McGavran and Win Arn[3]

whereby the potential for growth is greatly increased (see second column).

Addition	Multiplication
2	2
2 + 2 = 4	2 x 2 = 4
4 + 2 = 6	4 x 2 = 8
6 + 2 = 8	8 x 2 = 16
8 + 2 = 10	16 x 2 = 32
10 + 2 = 12	32 x 2 = 64
12 + 2 = 14	64 x 2 = 128
14 + 2 = 16	128 x 2 = 256
16 + 2 = 18	256 x 2 = 512

As a church works with God by building on the nine growth principles presented in this book, the potential for biblical church growth expands dramatically. Each principle essentially empowers other principles to the point that growth can explode. If a church uses only a few of the principles, there is some growth potential, but as a church builds its ministry with additional principles, its potential for growth accelerates.

The following three churches illustrate the multiplication effect.

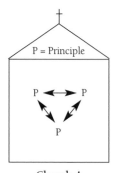

Church A

Church A above has only three of the biblical principles functioning well, which allows for very little growth potential. The church may hold a high view of the authority of God's Word (the right premise), seek to glorify God (the right priority), and be faithful in prayer (the right power), but the church may not see much numerical growth because it is not acting on the other six principles for biblical church growth.

In contrast, church B, with five growth principles in place, has a greatly increased potential for growth. Adding to the three principles found in church A, church B might also have a well-designed approach to discipleship (the right process) and effective leaders (the right pastors). The increased interaction created with the addition of two principles means church B has many times the growth potential of church A. Thus it is possible that church B, though it may have a confusing structure and be in a difficult location, could still grow due to the dynamic multiplication effect created by the five principles at work.

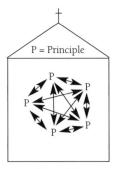

Church B

If all nine principles for biblical church growth are being used effectively, as in church C, an exponential multiplication effect is energized, often resulting in explosive growth.

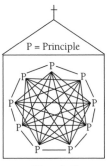

Church C

171

The reality, of course, is that no church has all nine principles fully functioning at top performance. Even churches that have all nine principles in place will discover that some may be more vital than others. Church growth is at once simple and complex because of the innumerable dynamics that mix together in a church. It is simple in that foundational biblical church growth principles can be identified. It is complex in that the mysterious working of the sovereign life-giving Spirit is always involved. Ultimately it is God who builds his church. It is our calling and joy to be fellow workers with him in the immense challenge of making disciples of all the nations.

A Growth Plan

Viewing a church as a web is a helpful way to visualize how the biblical principles of church growth are best developed. Principles at the center of the web are held tightly because they are the principles that provide the foundation for everything else. Principles at the periphery are held loosely, as they are not as central to the general structure of the web. Churches tend to grow best when they give priority to biblical principles of church growth from the center out. Organizational procedures are less important than having a firm biblical premise. Trusting in the Holy Spirit's power through prayer is of greater concern than knowing the target audience.

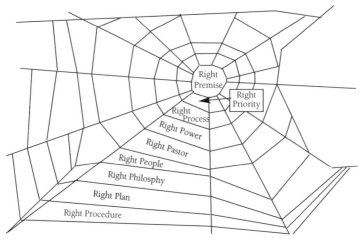

Therefore a growth plan should begin with the right premise, God's Word, and work outward to the right procedure, simple structure. Every church that desires to experience biblical church growth should consider the following steps.

Commit to the Right Premise: God's Word

The first biblical principle that church growth people emphasize is faithfulness to the plain meaning of the Bible, our authority. Church growth arises from theological roots and from biblical certainty. People of unshakable conviction can profitably employ insights from the many disciplines of common revelation—social sciences, management, and communication—but without biblical certainty all human resources become mere methods. The absolute certainty of the authority of the Word of God must be recaptured if the church is to be healthy and to fulfill its God-given purpose. Biblical church growth flows from absolute conviction that God desires to reconcile the world to himself and has commissioned his people to take the gospel to all the nations.

Among other things, churches desiring biblical church growth should

- submit themselves to the Bible as their only authority for faith and practice
- develop a clear understanding that men and women, boys and girls, are separated from God because of sin
- acknowledge that without a saving relationship with Jesus Christ, all people are destined to live eternally apart from God
- believe that Jesus Christ alone is the way to salvation and eternal life and that there is salvation in no one else
- return to the preaching and teaching of the ultimate, irrefutable, powerful Word of God

Focus on the Right Priority: Glorify God

The second biblical principle that church growth people emphasize is commitment to the ultimate goal of bringing glory to the life-

173

giving God. He is a glorious being who deserves honor, and it is part of our purpose as created beings to acknowledge God's unchanging attributes and life-giving nature. While there are many good ways to bring God glory—worship, praise, and living a godly life to name a few—a major means of bringing God glory is by bearing fruit. It is the very nature of God to give life to whatever he does. His life-giving purpose is revealed in the creation, in the establishment of his church, and, most important, in his reconciling work of redemption for all people. Churches that desire to experience biblical church growth cooperate with the life-giving God by bringing his life-giving gospel to lost people.

Among other things, churches desiring biblical church growth should

- acknowledge that God is the Creator and deserves honor and praise
- encourage public and private worship of God as a means of giving him glory
- develop ministries and programs that clearly seek to glorify God
- recognize that the primary means of giving glory to God is through bearing the fruit of new converts
- obediently place Christ's command to make disciples—bearing fruit that will remain—at the top of their priority list

Develop the Right Process: Discipleship

The third biblical principle that church growth people emphasize is the call to make disciples through a process of going, baptizing, and teaching. While bringing God glory is the ultimate goal of a local church, the immediate goal is to win people to faith in Christ. After winning them, it is essential to assimilate the new converts into the life of a local church and build them up in the faith by teaching them everything Christ commanded.

Among other things, churches desiring biblical church growth should

174

- develop an effective way to win people to faith in Christ
- design a process for welcoming, following up, and connecting newcomers to the life the local church
- organize a way to help believers mature in their faith through lifelong learning
- acknowledge that being a healthy church involves effectiveness in all three areas of going, baptizing, and teaching
- continually focus on developing these three areas of ministry

Trust in the Right Power: The Holy Spirit

The fourth biblical principle that church growth people emphasize is the sovereign work of the life-giving Holy Spirit for the growth of the church. Biblical church growth does not come through human effort but via the empowering ministry of the Holy Spirit. Accessing this power comes primarily through a life of prayer.

Among other things, churches desiring biblical church growth should

- publicly acknowledge reliance on the Holy Spirit for spiritual and numerical growth
- encourage the corporate and individual prayer life of the congregation
- actively pray for the growth of the church
- initiate prayer among the congregation for the salvation of the lost in the church community
- regularly seek God's face in prayer for the overall direction of the church

Follow the Right Pastor: A Faithful Shepherd

The fifth biblical principle that church growth people emphasize is following faithful under-shepherds in fulfilling the Great Commission. While we acknowledge that the Chief Shepherd is Jesus Christ, we recognize that he has appointed earthly shepherds to guide his church.

Among other things, churches desiring biblical church growth should

- select pastors who demonstrate a balance between character and competence
- encourage pastors to set the overall missional direction of the local church
- expect pastors to equip others to do the work of ministry rather than doing all the work themselves
- submit to the leadership of godly pastors as they seek to lead the church to fulfill the Great Commission
- organize teams of pastors to work together in serving the local body

Develop the Right People: Effective Ministers

The sixth biblical principle that church growth people emphasize is sacrificial service in life-giving ministry. If a church is serious about following Christ's commission to make disciples, all the people in the church must be involved. The church that sees the need of recruiting, training, and deploying people in ministry, and begins to do so, is way ahead of other churches in seeing biblical church growth take place.

Among other things, churches desiring biblical church growth should

- establish a plan to interview everyone in your church to determine his or her spiritual gifts, natural talents, and personal passions
- assist people to find a ministry that fits their God-given interests and provide for their on-the-job training
- recruit and deploy newcomers as quickly as possible while they are still excited about serving
- keep track of how many people are serving and in what ministries they are involved

176

- seek to deploy a minimum of 10 percent of all workers in the evangelism of non-Christians.

Use the Right Philosophy: Cultural Relevance

The seventh biblical principle church growth people emphasize is the need to relate to their communities in culturally relevant ways. While caution is warranted, a local church must adapt to culture in appropriate ways so that it remains in the world but not of the world.

Among other things, churches desiring biblical church growth should

- define their ministry area—how far will people likely travel to attend church?
- identify the community within the ministry area by analyzing population trends, family life and values, types of housing, ethnic makeup, economic and educational backgrounds of the people, and changes that are taking place
- determine what is open to change and what must remain the same in the church's ministry
- eliminate unnecessary barriers to communicating the gospel to people in the ministry area
- design new, culturally relevant ministries that will effectively communicate to and win new people to Christ from the community

Build the Right Plan: Target Focused

The eighth biblical principle church growth people emphasize is focusing on receptive people. A community is a mosaic of people, some of whom will be open and receptive to the gospel, while others will be closed and unreceptive to it. Faithful churches seek to discover the receptive people in their ministry area and focus their resources on them.

Among other things, churches desiring biblical church growth should

- identify receptive people in their ministry areas
- determine what part of the receptive mosaic God is preparing them to serve in the next few years
- focus primary efforts for outreach on near neighbors—receptive groups of people with similar lifestyles and backgrounds as the people already in the church
- focus church planting efforts on receptive groups of people who are very dissimilar to the church's congregation
- remain open to creative new methods and ministries that prove effective in winning new converts to Christ and assimilating them into the local church

Find the Right Procedure: Simple Structure

The ninth biblical principle that church growth people emphasize is the use of simple organizational systems. The Bible prescribes no clear organizational system for a local church; therefore it appears that a local church is free to develop an operating system that best fits the people and cultural context to which it ministers.

Among other things, churches desiring biblical church growth should

- analyze their current organizational structure to determine its weaknesses and strengths
- streamline their current organizational structure to eliminate unnecessary obstacles to church growth
- design new operating systems that allow the church to make quick ministry decisions without undue bureaucracy
- focus on maximizing ministry while minimizing maintenance
- concentrate on the function of ministry rather than the form of ministry

The Message of the Book

Biblical church growth is the heart and passion of the life-giving God. He sent his Son to be the life-giving Savior and empowered the

178

church through the life-giving Holy Spirit to take the gospel of salvation to the ends of the earth. Thousands upon thousands of illustrations throughout the Bible and in church history attest to the fact that God desires his church to grow and his lost children to be found. While the task of church growth remains primarily that of the Savior who declared that he would build his church, he also commanded that we be his coworkers in communicating his life-giving message to lost people in all the nations. I cannot do it, you cannot do it, but empowered by the life-giving Holy Spirit, we, the church, can do it!

Church growth is faithful obedience to God. It begins with acceptance of the Bible as the infallible, authoritative Word of God and continues with rock-ribbed conviction that God has opened only one way to salvation, through the shed blood of his Son on the cross and his resurrection from the dead on the third day. The battle for church growth is won or lost as these convictional foundations are accepted or rejected. People give themselves to and propagate what they believe to be eternally true. They are not willing to sacrifice time, energy, and effort to what they *think* may be true.

Once the convictional foundation is accepted, churches grow as they obediently put into place, through intentional strategies, the biblical principles of church growth discussed throughout this book. Church growth begins to become a reality as a process of discipleship is developed, the power of the Holy Spirit is tapped through prayer, and pastoral leaders are allowed to lead. When people in the church begin to minister sacrificially, when programs are designed to appropriately fit the culture of the community, and when the structure of the church maximizes ministry, then the potential for biblical church growth is dynamic.

The Crucial Question

With clear authority from God for church growth, the final question remains: Will we cooperate with God to build a faithful church? God has given us a mandate to make disciples so that he may be glorified. He has given us a life-giving message of hope for the world written in his life-giving Word. He has given us the life-giving Holy Spirit to empower us for service. He has given us life-giving principles for the growth of his church. Are we willing to work with him, as his coworkers, to reach the billions of people in the world who are yet to believe?

God wants his church to grow! He cares enormously for his lost sons and daughters throughout the world. Because God cares, we, his church, must care also. May God find us faithful as his coworkers for biblical church growth.

Lord, we give You thanks that You have called us to Your service in a day in which the Gospel is being proclaimed in a new way, with more vigor, with new hope and new effectiveness. Grant us, good Lord, wisdom and courage sufficient for these days, and grant that we serve honestly and intelligently. Deliver us from complaining. Make us sensitive to the leadings of Your Holy Spirit that we may play our part well in the revival and extension of Your church and the tremendous improvement of life which it is Your purpose to bring about. In Christ's blessed name we pray. Amen.

Donald A. McGavran[4]

Questions to Ask and Answer

1. What is your church's perspective on numerical church growth? What impact might this have on the future growth of your church?
2. Do the people in your church see numerical growth as a blessing or a problem? Do they desire to reach new people or would they prefer to remain at their current size?
3. Of the biblical church growth principles described in this book, which ones are functioning well in your church? Which ones are missing? Which ones are in place but functioning poorly?

4. Which principle do you think your church should begin focusing on in the next twelve months?
5. During your reading of this book, what ideas has God brought to your mind that your church needs to address in the coming year?

Postscript

The Great Denver Boat Race turned out to be a fine event for the youth groups that were involved. Not only did they have great fun, but they learned many lessons about working together, being creative, overcoming obstacles, and deferring to others when necessary.

Fortunately, the sponsors of the race had anticipated the failure of a few boats and positioned rescue boats on the lake to pick up the survivors (everyone survived, although most were quite wet)! Once everyone was safely on shore, a crowd gathered around the winning boat. They were not asking about the boat's unique design (it was the paddle wheeler), but they were asking, "How did you get your milk cartons to stay together?"

There was a lengthy discussion about how the boat was built. It was discovered that all the boats that lost milk cartons were made with water-soluble white paste glue. As the water splashed into the cracks between the milk cartons, the glue gradually softened until it was washed away, causing the cartons to separate. The builders of the winning boat, however, had used special contact cement that was impervious to water. When the waves splashed water into the cracks between the milk cartons, the glue held firm. The key was the glue!

The key to biblical church growth is also related to glue. The potential for churches to experience growth will be directly related to how effectively they are glued to the biblical principles of church growth. Some churches will seem to explode with growth and vitality, while others that appear to have potential will never get moving. Those that grow will be the ones that hold on tightly to the biblical principles of church growth. As churches submit to the life-giving Spirit and faithfully employ biblical principles, their potential for growth will accelerate.

Notes

Preface

1. Those unfamiliar with Donald McGavran should read *Understanding Church Growth,* 3d ed., rev. and ed. C. Peter Wagner (Grand Rapids: Eerdmans, 1990).

Chapter 1 Searching for Faithfulness

1. Charles Colson, *The Body* (Dallas: Word, 1992), 47.

2. Jim Cymbala, *Fresh Wind, Fresh Fire* (Grand Rapids: Zondervan, 1997), 124.

3. C. Peter Wagner, *Your Church Can Grow,* rev. ed. (Ventura, Calif.: Regal, 1984), 14.

4. Ralph D. Winter, "An Insider's View of McGavran," *Missions Frontiers* (June/October, 1990), 7.

5. Donald A. McGavran, tape collection 178, T39–19 January 1979 (Wheaton: Billy Graham Center Archives).

Chapter 2 The Life-Giving Church

1. While some local churches and church denominations do not baptize, the large majority of them do and see baptism as a prerequisite to being a member of a local church.

2. Donald A. McGavran, tape collection 178, T37–15 January 1979 (Wheaton: Billy Graham Center Archives).

Chapter 3 The Right Premise

1. For early studies on the place of biblical authority in church growth, see Donald A. McGavran and Winfield C. Arn, *Ten Steps for Church Growth* (San Francisco: Harper and Row, 1977) and *Back to Basics in Church Growth* (Wheaton: Tyndale, 1981). Examples of more recent studies are Thom Rainer, *Giant Awakenings* (Nashville: Broadman and Holman, 1995) and *Effective Evangelistic Churches* (Nashville: Broadman and Holman, 1996).

2. McGavran and Arn, *Back to Basics in Church Growth,* 13.

3. Reported by Kent R. Hunter in "Ask the Church Doctor," *Strategies for Today's Leader* 33, no. 2 (April/May/June), 13.

4. Donald A. McGavran, tape collection 178, T34–8 January 1979 (Wheaton: Billy Graham Center Archives).

Chapter 4 The Right Priority

1. Adapted from Glenn Van Ekeren, ed., "Never Lose Sight of Your Goals," *Words for All Occasions* (Paramus, N.J.: Prentice Hall, 1988), 188.

2. Westminster Shorter Catechism, question 1.

3. Lewis Sperry Chafer, *Systematic Theology* (Dallas: Dallas Seminary Press, 1948), 172.

4. James E. Rosscup, *Abiding in Christ* (Grand Rapids: Zondervan, 1973), 64.

5. Ibid., 67.

6. Leon Morris, *The Gospel According to John* (Grand Rapids: Zondervan, 1971), 672.

7. Rosscup, *Abiding in Christ,* 84.

8. Merrill C. Tenney, *John: The Gospel of Belief* (Grand Rapids: Eerdmans, 1948), 228.

9. The concept of "abide" is more complex than what is presented in this chapter. For brevity, I have used the basic understanding of the idea. For a full discussion of the word, see Rosscup's *Abiding in Christ,* chapter 11: "Things Involved in Abiding."

10. Donald A. McGavran, tape collection 178, T32–3 January 1979 (Wheaton: Billy Graham Center Archives).

Chapter 5 The Right Process

1. Those interested in a technical analysis of the Greek grammar are encouraged to see the following articles: Cleon Rogers, "The Great Commission," *BibliothecaSacra* 130, no. 519 (July/September 1973): 258–67; A. Boyd Luter Jr., "Discipleship and the Church," *BibliothecaSacra* 137, no. 547 (July/September 1980): 267–73; and J. Ronald Blue, "Go. Missions," *BibliothecaSacra* 141, no. 584 (October/Dec. 1984): 341–53.

2. For an excellent study of the Greek words *ethnos* and *ethne,* see chapter five, "The Supremacy of God among All the Nations," in John Piper, *Let the Nations Be Glad* (Grand Rapids: Baker, 1993), 167–218.

3. Donald A. McGavran, "Still Building the Bridges of God," an interview in *Global Church Growth* 21, nos. 4 and 5 (1984): 391.

4. Harvie Conn, ed., *Theological Perspectives on Church Growth* (New Jersey: Presbyterian and Reformed Publishing, 1977), 31.

5. Donald A. McGavran, "My Pilgrimage in Mission," *International Bulletin of Missionary Research* 10, no. 2 (1986): 57.

6. McGavran and Arn, *Ten Steps for Church Growth,* 57

7. Prayer adapted from *India Church Growth Quarterly* 5, no. 2 (1998): 10.

Chapter 6 The Right Power

1. Gordon MacDonald, *The Life God Blesses* (1994; repr., Nashville: Thomas Nelson, 1997), xix.

2. Richard Rigsby, "Not by Strategy, Not by Strength," *Talbot Times* 5, no. 9: 3.

3. Ibid.

4. Donald A. McGavran, *How Churches Grow* (London: World Dominion Press, 1959), 57.

5. McGavran and Arn, *Ten Steps for Church Growth,* 30.

6. Donald A. McGavran, "Ten Years of Church Growth Ministry in India," *India Church Growth Quarterly* 11, no. 2 (1989): 1.

7. McGavran, *How Churches Grow,* 55.

8. See Ray W. Ellis, "Spiritual Factors Impacting Church Health and Growth in the 21st Century," *Journal of the American Society for Church Growth* 10 (winter 1999): 3–22; and Marlin Mull, "Prayer and Church Growth," *Journal of the American Society for Church Growth* 11 (winter 2000): 69–77.

9. George W. Peters, *A Theology of Church Growth* (Grand Rapids: Zondervan, 1981), 49.

10. Carl F. George, *How to Break Growth Barriers* (Grand Rapids: Baker, 1993), 39.

11. Philip Van Auken, "Five Missing Ingredients," *Growing Churches* (April/May/June 1993), 57.

12. George, *How to Break Growth Barriers,* 38–39.

13. Adaptation of "Principles of Prayer" by Ralph Alexander, author's personal files, n.d.

14. Donald A. McGavran, tape collection 178, T33–5 January 1979 (Wheaton: Billy Graham Center Archives).

Chapter 7 The Right Pastor

1. See C. Peter Wagner, *Leading Your Church to Growth* (Ventura: Regal, 1984); and Wagner, *Your Church Can Grow,* 61–75.

2. Charles Van Engen, "Pastors as Leaders in the Church," *Theology, News and Notes* (June 1989): 15.

3. Gene Getz and Joe Wall, *Effective Church Growth Strategies* (Nashville: Word, 2000), 83.

4. Van Engen, "Pastors as Leaders in the Church," 16.

5. See Wagner, *Your Church Can Grow;* and Wagner, *Leading Your Church to Growth.*

6. Ted Engstrom and Ed Dayton, "Volunteers—Bane or Blessing?" *Christian Leadership Letter* (World Vision, May 1986), 2.

7. See Ray Gilder, "Your Church and Its Growth Vision," *Growing Churches* (October/November/December 1991): 24–25.

8. See F. W. Grosheide, "The First Epistle to the Corinthians" in the *New International Commentary on the New Testament,* 8th ed. (Grand Rapids: Eerdmans, 1976), 99.

9. H. A. Ironside, *Address on the First Epistle to the Corinthians* (New York: Loizeaux Brothers, 1938), 144.

10. McGavran, *How Churches Grow,* 181.

11. Donald A. McGavran, tape collection 178, T44 January 31, 1979 (Wheaton: Billy Graham Center Archives).

Chapter 8 The Right People

1. Kenneth Van Wyk, "Educate for Church Growth," *Church Growth: America* (March/April 1978), 8.

2. C. Peter Wagner, "Apostles and Intercessors," *Global Prayer News* 3, no. 3: 1.

3. Callahan, *Twelve Keys to an Effective Church,* 64.

4. Prayer adapted from *India Church Growth Quarterly* 5, no. 2 (1998): 9.

Chapter 9 The Right Philosophy

1. Charles Kraft, *Christianity in Culture* (New York: Orbis, 1979), 113.

2. Bill M. Sullivan, "A Multicultural Missionary Movement in North America," *GROW: A Journal of Church Growth, Evangelism and Discipleship* 3, no. 3: inside cover.

3. Elmer L. Towns, "You Can't Use Old Tools for Today's Job and Be in Business Tomorrow," *Fundamentalist Journal* (June 1984): 51.

4. George G. Hunter III, *Church for the Unchurched* (Nashville: Abingdon, 1996), 65.

5. For an interesting study of the biblical basis for adapting to culture, see Jerry E. Rueb, "Discovering Cultural Clues for Effective Evangelism in Suburbia" (D.Min. diss., Talbot School of Theology, May 1997).

6. Quoted in J. D. Douglas, *Let The Earth Hear His Voice* (Minneapolis: World Wide Publications, 1975), 101.

7. George G. Hunter III, *How to Reach Secular People* (Nashville: Abingdon, 1992), 67–68.

8. Towns, "You Can't Use Old Tools," 51.

9. Quoted in "Wisdom Words," *Ministries Today* (September/October 1996): 76.

10. Adapted from McGavran, tape collection 178, T45–2 February 1979 (Wheaton: Billy Graham Center Archives).

Chapter 10 The Right Plan

1. George G. Hunter III, quoted in *GROW: A Journal of Church Growth, Evangelism and Discipleship* 5 (1994): 13.

2. O. C. Emery, quoted in "Growth Markings and Main Points," *GROW: A Journal of Church Growth, Evangelism and Discipleship* 1 (1990): 5.

3. George G. Hunter III, quoted in *GROW: A Journal of Church Growth, Evangelism and Discipleship* 1 (1990): 5.

4. Lyle E. Schaller, *Innovations in Ministry* (Nashville: Abingdon, 1994), 51.

5. George G. Hunter III, quoted in "Growth Markings and Main Points," *GROW: A Journal of Church Growth, Evangelism and Discipleship* 4 (1993).

6. Adapted from a prayer in *India Church Growth Quarterly,* 13.

Chapter 11 The Right Procedure

1. Gary Martin and Gary McIntosh, *The Issachar Factor* (Nashville: Broadman and Holman, 1993), 81.

2. George Bullard, "Fuzzy Denominationalism: Learnings on Denominational Cultures," *Champions FAX* 2, no. 3 (Leadership Network, 10 February 1997): 1.

3. Adapted from a prayer given by Donald A. McGavran, tape collection 178, T52 February 1979 (Wheaton: Billy Graham Center Archives).

Chapter 12 Mix It Right

1. The words *auxano* (to grow) and *plethyno* (to multiply) are theologically significant since the same combination of terms is used in the LXX for the words *fruitful* and *multiply*. For a full discussion of the significance of these two words in the theology of Acts, see John Mark Hicks, "Numerical Growth in the Theology of Acts," *Journal of the American Society for Church Growth* 8 (spring 1997).

2. Ibid., 20.

3. McGavran and Arn, *Ten Steps for Church Growth,* 61.

4. Adapted from a prayer in tape collection 178, T58–9 March 1979 (Wheaton: Billy Graham Center Archives).

Scripture Index

189

Dr. Gary L. McIntosh is a nationally known author, speaker, consultant, and professor of Christian Ministry and Leadership at Talbot School of Theology, Biola University, located in La Mirada, California. He has written extensively in the field of pastoral ministry, leadership, generational studies, and church growth.

As president of the McIntosh Church Growth Network, a church consulting firm he founded in 1989, Dr. McIntosh has served more than 500 churches in 55 denominations throughout the United States and Canada. He was the 1995 and 1996 president of the American Society for Church Growth. Dr. McIntosh edits both the *Church Growth Network* newsletter and the *Journal of the American Society for Church Growth.*

Services Available

Dr. Gary L. McIntosh speaks to numerous churches, organizations, schools, and conventions each year. Services available include keynote presentations at major meetings, seminars and workshops, training courses, and ongoing consultation.

For a live presentation of the material found in *Biblical Church Growth* or to request a catalog of materials or other information on Dr. McIntosh's availability and ministry, contact:

The McIntosh Church Growth Network
P.O. Box 892589
Temecula, CA 92589-2589
909-506-3086
Email: cgnet@earthlink.net

On the World Wide Web at: www.mcintoshcgn.com
or www.churchgrowthnetwork.com